FULL LIST OF CONTRIBUTORS:

TAMAR ADLER · author of An Everlasting Meal

DANNY AMEND AND JOHN ADLER · Franny's and Marco's

NICK ANDERER · Maialino

JOSÉ ANDRÉS · chef/owner of ThinkFoodGroup

RYAN ANGULO · Buttermilk Channel

MICHAEL ANTHONY · Gramercy Tavern

DAN BARBER · Blue Hill and Blue Hill at Stone Barns

MARIO BATALI · Babbo Ristorante e Enoteca

JEREMY BEARMAN · Rouge Tomate

CHRIS BEISCHER · Mercer Kitchen

MARK BITTMAN · New York Times columnist and author of How to Cook Everything

APRIL BLOOMFIELD · The Spotted Pig

SAUL BOLTON · Restaurant Saul, The Vanderbilt, and Red Gravy

DANIEL BOULUD · DBGB Kitchen and Bar

SHARON BURNS-LEADER · Bread Alone

JOE CAMPANALE · dell'anima

MARCO CANORA · Hearth

JIMMY CARBONE · Jimmy's No. 43

CESARE CASELLA · Il Ristorante Rosi and Salumeria Rosi

MELISSA CLARK · New York Times columnist

MARY CLEAVER · The Green Table and The Cleaver Company

JOHN CONLIN · Tangled Vine

DANA COWIN · editor in chief at Food & Wine

KAREN DEMASCO · author of The Craft of Baking

GABLE ERENZO · Tuthilltown Spirits Distillers

FATTY CRAB

RICK FIELD · Rick's Picks

RON GALLO · JoJo

JACQUES GAUTIER · Palo Santo

CHESTER GERL · Hundred Acres

FANY GERSON · La Newyorkina

JOAN GUSSOW · author of This Organic Life

KURT GUTENBRUNNER · Wallsé

KERRY HEFFERNAN · author

SEAN HELLER · Momofuku Noodle Bar

AMY HESS · Northern Spy Food Co.

AMANDA HESSER · Food52.com and Provisions

PETER HOFFMAN · Back Forty and Back Forty West

JOEL HOUGH · Il Buco

DANIEL HUMM · Eleven Madison Park

SARA JENKINS · Porsena and Porchetta

MARCUS JERNMARK · Aquavit NYC

JENNIFER KING · Liddabit Sweets

ANNA KLINGER · al di la Trattoria

DAN KLUGER · ABC Kitchen

GABRIEL KREUTHER

RALF KUETT

MARK LADNER · Del Posto

RON LAPICO · Jean-Georges

DAVID LEBOVITZ · author of My Paris Kitchen

MATT LEE and TED LEE · authors of The Lee Bros. Charleston Kitchen

ED LEVINE · SeriousEats.com

STEVEN LINARES · Fort Defiance

BETH LINSKEY · Beth's Farm Kitchen

ANITA LO · Annisa

TOM MACY · Clover Club

PRESTON MADSON · Freemans

JIM MEEHAN · author of The PDT Cocktail Book

MARC MEYER · Cookshop

TIM MEYERS · Mas (farmhouse)

MARCO MOREIRA · Tocqueville

SEAMUS MULLEN · Tertulia

LIZ NEUMARK · Great Performances and Katchkie Farm

ROBERT NEWTON · Seersucker

PICHET ONG · pastry chef, blog pichetong.com

SISHA ORTUZAR · Riverpark

PEOPLE'S POPS

MICHAEL POLLAN · author of Cooked: A Natural History of Transformation

MIKE PRICE · Market Table

CARMEN QUAGLIATA · Union Square Café

RUTH REICHL · author of the novel Delicious!

ERIC RIPERT · Le Bernardin

CHARLES RODRIGUEZ · PRINT

ANTHONY SASSO · Casa Mono

AUDREY SAUNDERS · Pegu Club

LOUISA SHAFIA · author of The New Persian Kitchen

JUSTIN SMILLIE · Il Buco Alimentari & Vineria

JON SNYDER · Il Laboratorio del Gelato

MARTHA STEWART · Martha Stewart Living Omnimedia

BILL TELEPAN · Telepan & Telepan Local

SUE TORRES · Sueños

CHRISTINA TOSI · Momofuku Milk Bar

LIVIO VELARDO · Gotham Bar and Grill

CEDRIC VONGERICHTEN · Perry Street

DAVID WALTUCK · Ark Restaurants

JONATHAN WAXMAN · Barbuto

KAREN WEINBERG · 3-Corner Field Farm

REBECCA WEITZMAN · Thistle Hill Tavern

KENNETH WISS · Diner and Marlow & Sons

DAVID WONDRICH

MIKE YEZZI · Flying Pigs Farm

KATHERINE YOUNGBLOOD · Lot 2

THE NEW
Greenmarket
COOKBOOK

**RECIPES AND TIPS FROM
TODAY'S FINEST CHEFS**

**THE STORIES BEHIND THE
FARMS THAT INSPIRE THEM**

Gabrielle Langholtz

Da Capo
LIFE
LONG

A Member of the Perseus Books Group

Editorial production by Lori Hobkirk at the Book Factory.

Designed by Megan Jones Design.
Set in 10 point Brandon Grotesque by Megan Jones Design.

Cataloging-in-Publication data for this book is available from the Library of Congress.

First Da Capo Press edition 2014

ISBN: 978-0-7382-1689-8 (paperback)

ISBN: 978-0-7382-1690-4 (e-book)

Published by Da Capo Press
A Member of the Perseus Books Group
www.dacapopress.com

Da Capo Press books are available at special discounts for bulk purchases in the U.S. by corporations, institutions, and other organizations. For more information, please contact the Special Markets Department at the Perseus Books Group, 2300 Chestnut Street, Suite 200, Philadelphia, PA, 19103, or call (800) 810-4145, ext. 5000, or e-mail special.markets@perseusbooks.com.

10 9 8 7 6 5 4 3 2 1

To the people who sow seeds, pull weeds, carry water, nourish soils, pick rocks, tend flocks, lose crops, make cheese, catch fish, grind grain, hunt mushrooms, boil sap, get sunburned, get soaked, get stung, get bitten, get blisters, get tired, and get up so very early in the morning to feed New York City. And to the eaters who pay them to do so. Thank you.

Spring

Summer

Fall

Winter

Foreword

by **JAMES OSELAND,** EDITOR-IN-CHIEF OF *SAVEUR*

A bowl of Bosc pears was my introduction to the Union Square Greenmarket. It was a cold evening in the fall of 1980. I had just arrived on a visit from California—a seventeen-year-old with a growing interest in cooking and a boyfriend who lived on the Lower East Side. Michael had to work that night; he couldn't be home to greet me. Instead, in his tiny studio apartment I found those pears.

I picked up one and examined it. Misshapen, bird-pecked, and rough-skinned, the pear was so singular in its rough appearance that I found it beautiful. The supermarket pears I was accustomed to were perfect in color and form, but they smelled like nothing. Even at arm's length, this fruit had an aroma that was floral and intense. I took a bite; it was the sweetest pear I'd ever tasted. Then I noticed Michael's note wedged among the fruit: "I picked these up at the farmers market this morning. Welcome to New York. I love you."

Farmers market? Where in this big, crowded city were the farms?

"The market is in Union Square," Michael told me when he got home later that night, describing a collection of small family farmers who drove into the city from New Jersey and the Hudson Valley to sell produce there. "It runs all year. In winter, there's not much more than beets, onions, and apples. But it's the end of the fall harvest, and I found these."

It's hard to imagine now, but in 1980 New York was a radically different place. The Lower East Side was filled not with bistros and high-priced boutiques, but with vacant lots and piles of bricks where tenements once stood; a significant stretch of Avenue B was an open-air drug market. There were no café tables and big-box stores on Union Square; it was the Union Square conjured in the 1979 movie *The Warriors*, so gritty that it was easy to imagine rival gangs battling over its asphalt turf.

> *Even at arm's length, this fruit had an aroma that was floral and intense. I took a bite; it was the sweetest pear I'd ever tasted.*

A few days after my arrival, I went to see the Greenmarket for myself. There were just a few vendors back then, with folding tables holding cardboard boxes of ungainly, dirt-covered fruits and vegetables. But the young cook inside me was awakened by the place. There were enormous, primordial-looking cabbages. I bought one, so excited by the prospect of cooking it that I called my mother in California and asked her to read me some James Beard cabbage recipes over the phone.

That was more than three decades ago, and I still shop at the Greenmarket several times a week. It's no accident that, for as long as I've been in New York City, I have never lived more than a few minutes from it—today my apartment is two blocks away. I've watched the market grow from a small outpost to what

it is now: a multicolored, multiform phenomenon, an incomparable source for local produce and dairy, fish and meat, and baked goods. Without the market, New York would feel like an entropy to me; it's the center around which my life here revolves.

Like so many New Yorkers, I come to the market to shop, but I also walk through just to get inspiration from the world of ingredients, and to be reminded of the impressive human work that goes into bringing all that bounty to our city. In my relationship with the Greenmarket, I've grown from being a kid with a curiosity in food to a serious cook, a cookbook author, the editor of a food magazine. The Greenmarket has been immensely important to my own evolution—and likewise to New Yorkers and visitors of all stripes. It's a kind of magic that the Greenmarket holds, that even in this most urbanized of landscapes, we can eat a locally grown Bosc pear whose glorious taste can cause our experience of the world to shift.

Introduction

A NEW IDEA TAKES ROOT ON A CITY SIDEWALK

It began as an architect's experiment.

Nearly forty years ago, a visionary city planner named Barry Benepe set into motion something that would transform urban diets, rural economies, and the relationship between eaters and farmers in New York and, eventually, across the country. The idea was born when his work took him up to the Hudson Valley. There he saw hundreds of family farms in crisis—while just an hour's drive to the south, New Yorkers survived on insipid iceberg, mealy apples, and hard pink tomatoes: ingredients with about as much flavor as the Styrofoam they were packed in.

The Hudson Valley boasts some of the richest farmland in the country, but vegetable farms, dairy operations, and fruit orchards that a generation before had fed the Big Apple were losing their shirts, unable to compete with the giant industrialized farms that were shipping in cheap foods from distant lands. With no way to sell directly to New Yorkers, small family farmers upstate sold wholesale, watching middlemen take more and more of a cut, until wholesale prices fell so low that farmers, rather than lose money on each bushel, sometimes left their harvest to rot in the fields. In the twenty-five years between 1950 and 1974, two-thirds of New York State farms went out of business—and the state lost a staggering seven million acres of agriculture. Almost overnight, centuries-old farms were literally disappearing, making way for the march of suburban sprawl. Meanwhile, city dwellers downstate had all but forgotten the perfumed juice of a truly ripe peach or the inimitable crunch of sweet summer corn.

Benepe, on the other hand, couldn't forget. After a childhood divided between his parents' Gramercy Park apartment and grandfather's Maryland "truck farm," he knew the joy of eating tomatoes fresh off the vine, the challenge of selling them profitably, and the impossibility of finding anything in New York that tasted half as good. An experienced urban planner dissatisfied with the poor produce available in his otherwise amenity-rich metropolis, Benepe saw a single solution to the twofold problem of failing farms and undernourished urbanites. Urged on by the *New York Times*' John Hess, who famously thundered, "We don't need a study about farmers markets; we need farmers markets!" and with the help of a young planner named Robert Lewis, Benepe launched a project that would immeasurably improve the quality of life, upstate and down, for decades to come.

Opening day, 1976. (GrowNYC archives)

The response that first morning made the *Ed Sullivan Show* audience on the night of the Beatles' first appearance look lackluster by comparison. (GrowNYC archives)

After a year recruiting farmers (who thought Benepe and Lewis were crazy) and partnering with the Council on the Environment (later renamed GrowNYC), the duo eventually persuaded a dozen desperate farmers to load their harvest into pickups and bring it to a police parking lot in the shadow of the Queensboro Bridge. Urban farmers markets were altogether unheard of back in July of 1976, but the response that first morning made the *Ed Sullivan Show* audience on the night of the Beatles' first appearance look lackluster by comparison. As Dick Hodgson, one of the participating farmers, told writer John McPhee of that first day,

> The people were fifteen feet deep. There were just masses of faces. They went after the corn so fast I just dumped it on the ground. The people fell on it, stripped it, threw the husks around. They were fighting, grabbing, snatching at anything they could get their hands on. I had never seen people that way, never seen anything like it. We sold a full truck in five hours. It was as if there was a famine going on.

Nearly forty years later, GrowNYC's Greenmarket program now operates more than fifty markets across the city, and the farmers market phenomenon has taken the country by storm. According to the US Department of Agriculture (USDA), the number of US farmers markets rocketed from 1,700 in 1994 to 8,100 in 2013, as eaters nationwide have rediscovered the extraordinary flavors of food grown nearby on small family farms.

MARKETS TRANSFORM CITY LIFE

"If the Union Square Greenmarket were to leave my life, I would leave the city in a New York minute."
—**DANNY MEYER, UNION SQUARE HOSPITALITY GROUP**

The Greenmarket's opening day under the Queensboro Bridge was the start of a revolution. Benepe opened three more markets that summer: one in Harlem, one in downtown Brooklyn, and, on the edge of what was then known as Needle Park, the now-world famous location at Union Square.

Over the next thirty-five years, markets blossomed across the city. Today, Greenmarkets in operation from Jackson Heights to Bronx Borough Hall function as eaters' lifelines and village squares. Over the peas and peonies, otherwise-unapproachable city dwellers talk to strangers, set aside their differences, swap recipes, debate politics, and occasionally fall in love—in fact, a sociology study found that people are ten times as likely to talk to strangers at farmers markets as at supermarkets.

Farmers markets are at heart a social experience. Uninsured fisherman Rick Lofstadt once showed up to the Greenmarket with his arm in a sling only to have a customer (a surgeon) volunteer to operate on it for free. (The woman behind him happened to be an anesthesiologist and signed on to help as well). Maple syrup maker Andy Van Glad befriended a homeless crack addict and brought him upstate to get clean on

Over the corn and cabbage, New Yorkers set aside their differences. (GrowNYC archives)

(GrowNYC archives)

City dwellers had all but forgotten the perfumed juice of a truly ripe peach or the inimitable crunch of sweet summer corn. (GrowNYC archives)

The harvest is so diverse, you might say lettuce is just the tip of the iceberg. (Amanda Gentile)

the farm. After crises such as 9/11 and Superstorm Sandy, the markets offered New Yorkers comfort and camaraderie—and in the case of Sandy, processed food stamp sales when many powerless retailers could not. And at least three farmers have met their spouses at the market.

Stop a stranger at a farmers market and ask why she shops there, and she might say it's because the food on offer is better for the environment (small family farms are typically far more biodiverse, growing hundreds of crops rather than a single monocrop, and using more ecological growing methods—and transporting cantaloupe and cucumbers from a neighboring county, instead of another country, has a fraction of the carbon footprint). Or she might cite the health benefits of local food (which is picked at peak ripeness and often sold the day after harvest). But she's just as likely to name something more abstract: that it

just feels right to buy your food from the person who grew it, that the market is a place where she meets her community, that there's something reassuring about traceability, something deeply meaningful about eating this way, and that participating in a human-scale food system adds richness to life.

These real-life, feel-good experiences are a welcome antidote to the seemingly endless stream of disturbing reports about our food industry. Even when there's not an outbreak of E. coli (in organic spinach, no less!) or avian flu or mad cow disease, the everyday evils of industrial agriculture have brought on a plague of "diabesity," created a dead zone the size of Massachusetts in the Gulf of Mexico, and set this generation on track to be the first in American history with a shorter life expectancy than their parents. Against this backdrop of grim news, farmers markets abound with community connections and culinary collaborations.

FARMERS RISE TO THE OPPORTUNITY

"If it weren't for Greenmarket, I'd be selling used cars." —**FARMER ANDY VAN GLAD**

An utter transformation of American agriculture took place after World War II. The embrace of industrial agriculture devastated small family farming—and the American diet. Prized heirloom varieties of vegetables and heritage breeds of livestock went the way of the dodo bird. As USDA policy urged farmers to "get big or get out," by planting hedgerow to hedgerow, food became cheap—but at great social, environmental, and public health cost.

The founding of the Greenmarket offered small family farms a ray of hope. Instead of selling mono-culture commodities (such as onions, apples, or dairy) for pennies on the dollar, local farms were now able to sell direct through the Greenmarket and make a real living growing high-quality food.

Farmer Ron Binaghi Jr. was only sixteen on the first day he came to the Greenmarket in 1976, and he vividly remembers money being thrown at him by city folk starved for fresh produce. One of a dozen "first family" Greenmarket farmers still selling today, Binaghi's multigenerational farm family is part of a breed of growers who realized that in order to keep themselves in business, they'd have to biodiversify their crops for the growing demands of hungry urban-ites and the chefs who serve them. Ron recalls, "When a customer asked us, 'Do you grow chamomile?' we didn't know what it was, but we said, 'We'll find out, and we'll grow it.'" Binaghi's New Jersey farm went from growing just four crops to more than eighty, thanks to his vow that if customers want it, he'll find a way to get it onto their plates. Fortunately history repeats itself: Although the average American farmer is now

over age fifty-five, Binaghi's son, Ron III, inherited his father's attitude, saw a viable future in raising food for city shoppers, and is now carrying on the tradition at the twice-weekly Greenmarket at Lincoln Center.

Barry Benepe knew the joy of eating tomatoes fresh off the vine, the challenge of selling them profitably, and the impossibility of finding anything in New York that tasted half as good.

Farmers markets have given growers a way out of the industrial treadmill, which leads to fields of mono-cultures, fetid factory farms, manure lagoons and a poisoned environment. Freed from the tyranny of the corporate food system, small family farmers (who drink the well water and plan to pass their land to their children) favor ecological production methods—or-ganic (whether certified or not), as well as biodynamic (which builds upon the teachings of Austrian philoso-pher Rudolf Steiner), Integrated Pest Management (which treats for pests only when vital and at the pre-cise moment of maximum opportunity, thus vastly reducing chemical use), and mineralization (which decomposes or oxidizes chemical compounds into plant-accessible forms in the soil). These independent farmers also embrace pasture-based or grass-fed

Selling direct allows a transition from commodity agriculture to a human-scale system. (Amanda Gentile)

livestock production, which forgoes the diet of corn and antibiotics, instead returning herbivores such as sheep and cows to the fields of grass, and putting pigs in the woods where they can root to their porcine hearts' delight.

At the same time that market participants are employing specific ecological practices to create their unique products, some fishers, foragers, and farmers are creating new markets for little-known edibles, such as Northshire Farm's forest-found morels and porcini, Blue Moon Fish's tunny and sea robin (which other fishers would throw back, dead), and Roaming Acres' delectable ostrich and emu meat. These innovations ask shoppers to open their minds and mouths to species they may never have tasted—or seen.

Production methods aren't the only things improving, and independent farmers aren't simply maintaining their corner of an otherwise-crumbling foodshed. Through Greenmarket, some farmers are working to reinvent a component of the food system. Wild Hive Farm and Cayuga Pure Organics are reviving the local grain economy. An increasing number of midsize growers are selling additional ingredients through Greenmarket Co., GrowNYC's mission-driven wholesale operation, which provides a competitive retail price to bigger farmers who are happy to sell their chard or cilantro by the box, not the bunch.

Farmers markets enabled many families to transition from failing commodity agriculture into a reimagined human-scale system. This has brought about a combination of old and new, of legacy and innovation, of horse-drawn plows and electric livestock fencing, a renaissance of growing grain and a heyday of artisan alcohol.

CULTIVATING ECOLOGICALLY AWARE EATERS

A keystone program of GrowNYC—a nonprofit organization dedicated to creating a healthier and more sustainable New York City—Greenmarket creates centers for citizens to participate in environmental restoration.

You might say local lettuce is just the tip of the iceberg. The Greenmarkets are more than just a place to pick up tonight's dinner ingredients. Answering a call from customers who wanted to dispose of their food waste in an environmentally sound way, in 2011, GrowNYC launched a compost initiative that diverted more than 1 million pounds of kitchen scraps from the waste stream in its first year. Customers can buy their carrots at Greenmarket, then bring the peels and tops back to be composted. These are then transformed into a fertile soil amendment for use in local urban farming and gardening projects. With the help of the City of New York, the number of Greenmarket collection sites has expanded and has led to the sanitation department initiating composting programs in schools and neighborhoods across the city.

Similarly, customers can bring their old clothing and textiles to market to be recycled. Since GrowNYC began its textile recycling program in 2007, more than 2 million pounds of old clothing, shoes, linens, handbags, and other textiles have been collected—putting landfills on a diet.

But the good work isn't only happening at Greenmarket. GrowNYC also operates environmental education, recycling, and community garden programs across New York. The organization is growing green spaces in our neighborhoods, growing public awareness about conservation and recycling, and—most importantly—growing young people who are better educated about environmental issues and leaders in their communities.

The project would immeasurably improve the quality of life, upstate and down, for decades to come.

GrowNYC programs for kids range from the Randall's Island Urban Farm (a 3,000-square-foot learning garden that invites school groups to grow, harvest and eat garden-fresh produce) to Learn It Grow It Eat It (a South Bronx high school initiative that pays teenagers to tend organic fruit, vegetables, and herbs in three local community gardens, run a weekly farm stand, and teach children and adults about the environment and healthy eating). And to provide large-scale support to school gardens citywide, GrowNYC is a founding partner of Grow to Learn NYC, a comprehensive program to organize all school garden efforts.

FOOD ACCESS AND JUSTICE

The local food movement is sometimes cast as an elite way to eat, typified by the wealthy urbanite who buys edible flowers to scatter across the grass-fed steak at her dinner party. And while people with means are among the Greenmarket's many customers, they shop alongside New Yorkers of all walks of life.

In fact, many farmers report that their highest sales aren't at Union Square, but in lower-income neighborhoods where recent immigrants eat in every night, often cooking for extended families. The Greenmarket has long worked to provide a continuing supply of fresh local food to all New Yorkers, and in the early 2000s has been a critical civic ally in increasing food access in underresourced neighborhoods.

Greenmarket's Food Stamps in Farmers Markets initiative serves as a national model. When the USDA transitioned from paper coupons to debit card–style EBT (electronic benefits transfer) cards, the shift didn't just reduce stigma and fraud—it also inadvertently left farmers markets, which typically lack landlines and electricity, on the wrong side of the digital divide. Ironically, citizens with the greatest food insecurity could buy candy bars and soda at the corner bodega but were unable to redeem their benefits on spinach or squash at the neighborhood farmers markets—until Greenmarket cofounder Bob Lewis, who had a long career at the New York State Department of Agriculture, piloted wireless EBT terminals.

As word spread, the crowds swelled, and the benefits to upstate and urban communities alike have been exponential. In 2012, the markets processed over $800,000 in EBT sales. The Union Square market alone saw $241,000 in EBT sales. Two-dollar market coupons called Health Bucks, originally created by the Department of Health to help at-risk communities eat more produce, now stretch Supplemental Nutrition Assistance Program (SNAP) sales at Greenmarket. For *every* $5 purchase, SNAP shoppers receive one $2 Health Buck, resulting in a 40 percent boost in buying power. In an era of angry debate about whether sugar-sweetened beverages should be eligible for SNAP purchase—they currently account for a staggering $4 billion a year in Food Stamp sales—Health Bucks offer a stimulus, rather than restriction. And while Greenmarket's program is the nation's largest city-operated SNAP, $16.6 million of SNAP benefits were used at farmers markets nationwide in 2012, up from $7.5 million in 2010, thanks to the growing availability of EBT terminals at markets.

In 2012, Greenmarket processed more than $800,000 in food stamp sales (Jameel Khaja)

CHEFS MAKE CRUCIAL CONNECTIONS

"If this is your first visit to the market, you're in for the most delicious experience of your life."
—CHEF PETER HOFFMAN, BACK FORTY AND BACK FORTY WEST

Each market day in summer and fall, more than five hundred thousand New Yorkers shop at the Greenmarket—a number that includes scores of the country's best cooks. In the early hours, the bright red chard, orange squash, and purple kale are contrasted with the crisp white of jackets, as chefs finger speckled cranberry beans, sniff fresh anise hyssop, and select Cherokee Purple tomatoes to buy by the case—God help the taxi they'll hail. Lured by the call of superior flavor, many have developed close business relationships—and even close friendships—with the men and women whose food forms their kitchens' foundations. Thanks to the Greenmarket, scores of the city's top toques and celebrity chefs have become ardent advocates of sustainable agriculture, collaborating with farmers to transform the way New York eats.

They're here because the farmers have learned to entice them with ingredients that easily elevate any menu, and those pros in turn commission farmers to grow old varieties and raise little-known breeds so flavorful they're worth their weight in gold—and chefs are willing to pay accordingly.

Today's farm-to-table craze began back in the 1980s with a few early handshakes between palms calloused by hoe handles and fingers scarred by scrapes with stoves. It was all born of eager, innovative farmers, such as Rick Bishop of Mountain Sweet Berry Farm, who saw an opportunity to think outside the commodity box. Despite the American agricultural experts' insistence that profits lay in high yields of varieties that could withstand long-distance transport,

Chefs like Peter Hoffman have taught their patrons to look askance at apricots before August. (Amanda Gentile)

Bishop favored flavor. He built up his soils with minerals and sought out unique varieties—like his signature Tristar strawberry, which is a domestic strawberry crossed with a wild alpine strain and whose tiny fruits taste like strawberries straight from God's own garden. Cooks soon swarmed his stand and Bishop confirmed his hunch—that they were starved for interesting ingredients, and that taste was the path to profit.

Pastured livestock production returns herbivores to fields of grass.

Chefs found Bishop was game to grow special requests. David Bouley, for example, longed for French Lyonnais potatoes like those from his hometown and gave Bishop $10,000 to develop seed stock and enrich his soil to grow purple Peruvian and ruby crescent potatoes. And lo, the fingerling craze swept American ovens. Chef Cesare Casella brought the farmer nineteen heirloom varieties of shell beans from Tuscany—and Bishop grew every last one.

This symbiotic relationship has blossomed like a sunflower. Many chefs have even made the pilgrimage to Bishop's Catskill kingdom to read seed catalogs, dig potatoes, savor strawberries, and forage for ramps and fiddleheads with their Greenmarket guru. Mere mortals shop his tiny stand, too, landing the likes of celtuse, which tastes something like a cross between celery and lettuce, and, come winter, tiny crunchy

tubers called crosnes that look like miniature Michelin men and just might land you a Michelin star.

It's not only Bishop. Call today's culinary moment the "cult of the ingredient." What began with Bouley and Bishop back in the 1980s has, over time, ushered out the dusty culinary era of commodities lost in white French sauce. As chefs sank their teeth into real produce, they threw off those béchamel blankets and put the spotlight on the ingredients. The trend has coalesced into menus that read like seed catalogs.

Drawing on taste-memories of unforgettable fruits from a backyard cherry tree, or dreaming up flavor profiles based on an herb they only just met, cooks cast local ingredients in preparations from European classics to reimagined homey American fare to cutting edge molecular gastronomy. Across the board, these chefs have turned their training on its head, and mastered the art of writing last-minute menus after a morning at the market—sometimes just moments before unlocking the door for dinner. And on those pages it has become standard practice to list farm names below each dish. Enlightened chefs have trained their diners to eat asparagus only in May, to look askance at apricots before August, and even to expect that burgers shall remain tomatoless for eight months each year.

Nearly forty years later, the Greenmarket operates more than fifty markets, and the phenomenon has taken the country by storm.

This book embodies the experience of life at market. You'll find recipes ripe for each season, direct from the chefs and food artisans who know their farmers. Profiles of the growers themselves take you to upstate New York, where a city-raised former nurse discovered that the secret to true nourishment is in soil; to the Connecticut countryside, where one family tends generations of cows that bring farmstead cheese to city dwellers; and to Long Island, where a husband/wife team who first met at market make their life by fishing and selling their catch directly to customers. But you needn't be a New Yorker to cook from this book. From Boston to Austin, Seattle to Savannah, farmers markets have put down roots across the country. On city sidewalks and grassy fields, these seemingly simple marketplaces benefit ecology, economy, and community. They also offer the real peaches and corn Barry Benepe dreamed of decades ago.

See you there.

Spring

ANCHOVY BUTTER ON TURNIPS

by **MELISSA CLARK, DINING SECTION COLUMNIST,** *NEW YORK TIMES*

After a winter of braised or roasted turnips from the root cellar, the spring crop seems like another vegetable altogether—one that you can't resist eating raw. Buy them with their tops attached, and you know the little roots will be crunchy and sweet. Here Melissa Clark whips up a simple herb butter to slather on them. This recipe makes a big batch of the butter, far more than you'll eat with one bunch of turnips. You can easily halve or quarter the quantities, but it freezes just fine and is also fantastic on chicken or steak.

½ CUP (1 STICK) UNSALTED BUTTER, ROOM TEMPERATURE

6 FINELY MINCED ANCHOVY FILLETS

1 MINCED SCALLION

1 TABLESPOON MINCED DILL

1 MINCED GARLIC CLOVE

¼ TEASPOON KOSHER SALT, OR TO TASTE

¼ TEASPOON FRESHLY GROUND BLACK PEPPER

1 TABLESPOON LIME JUICE

1 BUNCH TINY TURNIPS, CLEANED AND TRIMMED

In a bowl, mash together the butter, anchovies, scallion, dill, garlic, salt, pepper, and lime juice. Mix well and add more salt and/or lime juice to taste. Spread the mixture on the turnips.

SERVES 4 TO 6

DILL PICKLED RAMPS

by **DANIEL HUMM, ELEVEN MADISON PARK**

2 POUNDS RAMPS

3 CUPS WHITE VINEGAR

1½ CUPS LOOSELY PACKED DILL

6 TABLESPOONS SALT

2 TABLESPOONS DILL SEEDS

2 TEASPOONS CORIANDER SEEDS

2 TEASPOONS RED CHILI FLAKES

2 PEELED GARLIC CLOVES

Plenty of Greenmarket ingredients inspire obsession, from goose eggs to chanterelles to quince. But if you ask any farmer or chef to name the single greatest cult crop at market, you'll likely get a one-word reply: ramps.

Looking like a little version of their domestic cousin the leek, this wild allium appears in the forest—and at market and on menus all over town—shortly after the ground thaws each spring. To extend ramp season beyond the few weeks they're foraged, Chef Daniel Humm preserves them as quick "refrigerator" pickles, which he suggests serving alongside steak, on a charcuterie platter, or even as a topping for hot dogs.

You can also add a few to the Casa Mono salad dressing (page 45). Save the leafy green tops for David Waltuck's Fresh Fettuccine with Spring Greens (page 43).

Trim and discard any roots from the ramps. Remove the leafy green tops and reserve for another purpose. You'll be left with the white bulbs, plus about one inch of the pink stem. Divide them between two clean 2-quart glass jars.

In a medium stockpot, combine the remaining ingredients with 3 cups of water. Bring to a boil, stir to dissolve the salt, and pour over the ramps. Allow to cool to room temperature before covering. Refrigerate at least one week; keep up to one month.

MAKES 2 QUARTS

DANDELION GREEN SALAD WITH MARKET PANCETTA

by **ANNA KLINGER, AL DI LA TRATTORIA**

3 OUNCES PANCETTA (OR 3 TO 4 SLICES OF THICK-CUT BACON), DICED INTO ¼-INCH CUBES

1 TEASPOON PLUS 2 TABLESPOONS EXTRA VIRGIN OLIVE OIL, DIVIDED

3 TABLESPOONS SHERRY VINEGAR

6 OUNCES DANDELION GREENS (ABOUT 1 SMALL BUNCH), WASHED AND DRIED, THICK STEMS REMOVED

SALT AND FRESHLY GROUND BLACK PEPPER

Dandelion's name comes from the French *dent de lion* (dragon's tooth), a nod to the leaves' jagged edges. Some growers gather wild dandelion in March, before the leaves become prohibitively bitter. These wild greens can serve as a tonic—a bodily "spring cleaning" after a long winter of rich meals.

But you don't need to save this recipe for those weeks of the year. As the weather warms, several farmers cultivate a type of chicory, long popular in Italian cooking, labeled "dandelion." Either the wild dandelion or the cultivated chicory will work well in this recipe, as can their cousin, puntarelle.

This deliciously simple salad can be turned into a main dish by crowning it with a poached egg.

In a small sauté pan over low heat, cook the diced pancetta in one teaspoon of olive oil until it has browned lightly and rendered out much of its fat. This should take 7 to 8 minutes and yield about 4 tablespoons of fat.

Remove the pan from the heat and allow the pancetta to cool slightly. Add the sherry vinegar and remaining 2 tablespoons of olive oil. Set aside and keep warm.

Place the dandelion greens in a large mixing bowl, season lightly with salt and pepper, and pour the warm pancetta vinaigrette over the greens. With your hands, massage the dressing into the greens, which will help to tenderize them and meld the flavors of the vinaigrette and the greens.

Serve warm.

SERVES 4

ARAUCANA

DUCK

ARAUCANA

TURKEY

DUCK

PHEASANT

PHEASANT

GOOSE

PHEASANT

PHEASANT

ARAUCANA   PHEASANT

Farmer NEVIA NO
BODHITREE FARM

Nevia No was forty when she first set foot on a farm, but in the few intervening years—today she barely looks forty-one—she quickly became known for the most beautiful farm stand anywhere.

Although Nevia wasn't born into farming, she did grow up around food. Back in Seoul, South Korea, her mother's family ran one of the largest, most famous restaurants in the country. But despite her urban up-bringing, Nevia says that, even as a child, she felt inside that she needed to live on a farm. Her grandfather's garden pots on the cement rooftop made her happy, but beyond that, farming was an impractical dream.

Instead she trained in the performing arts—dance, piano, cello, and eventually studying voice at a con-servatory of music—but she never forgot that unre-alistic dream, and, through what she calls unconscious movement, life eventually led her to the land. Today she owns 65 acres in New Jersey. The sandy soil is surrounded by preserved pine forests, which she says offer a strong, serene energy. She named the farm Bodhitree after the spiritual tree under which the Buddha found enlightenment.

Many eaters find enlightenment at her stand, in the form of picture-perfect rare and heirloom veg-etables. Some are of Asian extraction, such as her Korean chameh melon, "avocado" summer squash, shiso leaf, seedless cucumbers, daikon radish, pur-ple Japanese sweet potatoes, and shishito blister-ing roasting peppers, which is a Japanese cousin of Spain's celebrated *padrons*. But she also grows Bordeaux spinach, red and purple okra, multicolored

◀ *Nevia trained in dance, piano, cello, and voice but says unconscious movement led her to the land.* (Amanda Gentile)

cauliflower, a spectacular array of heirloom tomatoes, and an abundance of beans—fava, broad, and shell—with names like Mayflower and Calypso.

"I try to grow things that other people don't grow—don't even dare to grow," she explains. "Hard-to-grow crops really challenge me. If I'm the only person with something, that really gives me a sense of accomplishment."

And while she wasn't trained in agriculture, she has spent recent years studying, reading, and learning. The fruits of her labor arrive at market in the form of uncommon crops such as *agretti*, a green native to the Mediterranean coast that has a wonderful crunchiness and natural saltiness but is very difficult to germinate here. In fact, many of Nevia's crops are so unusual that chefs don't know how to prepare them. She and her mother experiment in the kitchen, so at market, she can give recipes to the world's best cooks.

She named the farm Bodhitree after the spiritual tree under which the Buddha found enlightenment.

Sometimes chefs return from travels with requests for specific varieties, such as the crisp Fushimi pepper she now grows. "I didn't know anything about it," she recalls, "but I said, 'Bring me the seeds.'"

She says she farms through instinct rather than intellect. "I wasn't technically trained, so I don't know what I'm doing, but I *feel* what I'm doing. I can communicate with the plants, feel their energy, feel what they need."

And she puts her arts training to a new use. "Now I use my music education on plants. When I'm on the tractor, I sing arias. I pray, I meditate, I talk to the plants, saying 'Here is the music, I love you, please return what I'm giving to you.' I have a belief that they can hear and feel me."

Plants that don't meet her own needs do not make it to market—and Nevia is a perfectionist. "People always ask, 'How does everything grow so beautifully?' They don't understand. I bring in about 40 percent of what I grow. The rest goes to chicken feed or compost."

Few farmers would discard half their yield, but Nevia holds herself to a different standard. "For me, beauty is the most important aspect. If something doesn't satisfy my eyes, first I wouldn't want to put it in my mouth. Not everyone is my customer, but I can pick out the ones who share my appreciation of beauty."

In that spirit, she covers her market tables with white tablecloths. In the early days she recalls other farmers walked by laughing, saying, "Do you think this is Saks Fifth Avenue?" But she felt the contrast showed her harvest's beautiful colors, and today other farmers follow suit.

But don't confuse her love of beauty with effeteness. "I am a very tough person inside," says Nevia. "If you're not super disciplined, this is not something you could do, regardless of your gender. I get up at four in the morning, and in the summer I work twenty hours a day. Of course it's exhausting, physical work every day, nonstop, no rest. I cannot say it's a comfortable life, physically, but it is very spiritual and soulful. The energy from the earth and nature, plants and the air, it pulls me back to do this hard life again, thinking how to make it even better and more beautiful. I don't want to do anything else besides this."

ASPARAGUS MILANESE

by **MARIO BATALI, BABBO RISTORANTE E ENOTECA**

SALT

20 JUMBO ASPARAGUS SPEARS, TOUGH ENDS SNAPPED OFF

6 TABLESPOONS EXTRA-VIRGIN OLIVE OIL, DIVIDED

FRESHLY GROUND BLACK PEPPER

2 DUCK EGGS

GRATED PARMIGIANO-REGGIANO, OR A FIRM, AGED GOAT CHEESE, FOR SERVING

This dish is a riff on a recipe that's been served at Babbo for years. You can use any egg, but precious duck eggs are an annual delicacy for their pretty shells, speckled like wrens', and their wonderfully humongous yolks.

Everyone knows that asparagus is a sign of spring, but eggs are, too. Although chickens have been bred to lay eggs all year long, farmed ducks, pheasants, turkeys, and geese lay when the days are getting longer, just as their wild ancestors always have. And that means interesting eggs are abundant during asparagus season—especially at the stand of Carmella Quattrociocchi of Quattro's Game Farm, who has been keeping game birds since 1944, when she was twelve, and can identify each egg by taste as well as sight. The shell indicates the breed, while the yolk belies the bird's diet—pastured poultry lay eggs with deep orange yolks.

Bring 3 quarts of water to a boil and add 1 tablespoon of salt. Prepare an ice bath. Blanch the asparagus in the boiling water for 1 minute and 30 seconds, then remove and immediately refresh in the ice bath. Once cooled, remove the asparagus from the ice bath with tongs and pat dry. Set aside.

In a large sauté pan, heat 3 tablespoons of olive oil over high heat. Add the asparagus and toss in the oil over high heat for 1 minute, season with salt and pepper, then divide evenly among two warmed plates.

Wipe out the sauté pan with a paper towel, add the remaining 3 tablespoons of oil, then heat over medium-high heat. Crack the eggs into the pan, taking care not to break the yolks. Cook the eggs sunny side up until the whites are firm but the yolk is still runny, about 2 to 3 minutes. Season each egg with salt and pepper, then carefully slide 1 egg onto each of the asparagus servings. Shave a generous helping of cheese over each plate and serve immediately.

SERVES 2

OYSTERS ON THE HALF SHELL
WITH RHUBARB MIGNONETTE

by **ANITA LO, ANNISA**

**1 OUNCE FINELY DICED RHUBARB
(ABOUT 2 TABLESPOONS)**

**1 SMALL, FINELY DICED SHALLOT
(ABOUT 1 TABLESPOON)**

**½ TEASPOON CRACKED BLACK
PEPPER**

3 TABLESPOONS WHITE BALSAMIC

SALT TO TASTE

**12 WELL-CHILLED OYSTERS,
SCRUBBED CLEAN**

CHOPPED CHIVES, FOR GARNISH

Why pay three dollars apiece for oysters at a raw bar when they can be had, pristinely fresh and plump in their shells, for fifty cents each? That's about how much Long Island fishers charge for these silky opalescent bivalves, pulled from the Sound nets where they're sustainably raised. Sure, some aquaculture is environmentally problematic, but farmed oysters actually restore wild waters—up to two gallons can pass through each specimen per hour as it feasts on phytoplankton and processes nitrogen.

Learn to shuck your own, and you'll feast for life. An oyster knife only costs a few bucks; some people also gain access with a butter knife or a flathead screwdriver. Chef Anita Lo, who weekends out on Long Island and catches her own seafood on the coast, says it's true that chilling oysters until they're ice cold—but not actually frozen—makes shucking easier, as the little bivalves relax and don't hold their shells quite so tightly closed. Scrub them well, wrap your "weak" hand in a towel to avoid shucking yourself, and hold the oyster flat side up so you won't spill those ethereal liquors within. Now pry the hinge open—it shouldn't take too much force. Once you've sprung it, slide your blade along the top shell to cut the abductor muscle. Some love the silky-sweet meat straight, but this rhubarb mignonette is a beautiful way to gild the lily.

Mix the rhubarb, shallot, black pepper, and white balsamic with 1 tablespoon of water and season to taste with the salt. Shuck the oysters, place a small amount of mignonette on each (or serve alongside) and garnish with the chopped chives.

WARM MUSHROOM SALAD WITH FAVA BEANS

by **REBECCA WEITZMAN, THISTLE HILL TAVERN**

You know that old adage about how you have to break a few eggs to make an omelet? Well if you want to make this dish, you're going to have to shell some fava beans—twice—but it's worth it. While some faux-farmy restaurants plop imported favas on their menus as early as March, the real thing isn't ripe in the Northeast until June, when the fat, foamy, freckled pods arrive at market. Buy a lot, because they're mostly pod.

Yes, favas require some effort—first each pod must be split open and the little gray-green beans plucked out, then after a quick blanching, each individual fava must have its pale jacket nicked and slipped off. While it's not something you'll find yourself making for a quick snack, the payoff is real, and you can recruit your guests to help.

Fresh favas are magnificent with just a drizzle of oil and a pinch of salt, but here they share the stage with meaty wild mushrooms, all finished with a shower of fresh herbs.

Bring a small saucepan of water to a boil and season it well with salt. Blanch the shelled fava beans for 2 minutes. Drain and rinse under cold water until chilled. Pop the beans out of their skins and set aside.

Heat a 12-inch sauté pan over medium-high heat until very hot. Add 3 tablespoons of olive oil, and when it shimmers, add the sliced mushrooms in a single layer and sear until lightly browned on one side, about 2 minutes. Turn to evenly cook the other side to a golden brown, about 2 more minutes. Reduce heat to low and add the peeled fava beans, hazelnuts, onions, thyme, and balsamic vinegar. Toss until the onions are just wilted, 1 to 2 minutes, then remove from heat and add parsley, mint, salt, and pepper. Finish with Parmesan, the remaining 1 tablespoon of olive oil, lemon juice, and fresh cracked black pepper.

SERVES 2 TO 4

½ CUP SHELLED FAVA BEANS, FROM ABOUT 7 TO 8 LARGE PODS

4 TABLESPOONS EXTRA VIRGIN OLIVE OIL, DIVIDED

2 CUPS SLICED WILD MUSHROOMS (ANY VARIETY THAT ARE IN SEASON), ABOUT ½-INCH THICK

¼ CUP HAZELNUTS, TOASTED AND ROUGHLY CHOPPED

5 SPRING ONIONS, WHITE AND GREEN PARTS, THINLY SLICED

1 TEASPOON FRESH THYME LEAVES

2 TABLESPOONS BALSAMIC VINEGAR

¼ CUP WHOLE PARSLEY LEAVES

¼ CUP ROUGHLY CHOPPED MINT LEAVES

SALT AND FRESHLY GROUND BLACK PEPPER

4 TABLESPOONS SHAVED PARMESAN, OR OTHER HARD, AGED CHEESE

2 TABLESPOONS LEMON JUICE, FROM ABOUT 1 LEMON

PUNTARELLE THREE WAYS

by **RUTH REICHL, AUTHOR OF THE NOVEL** *DELICIOUS!*

The Classic

1 HEAD PUNTARELLE

1 GARLIC CLOVE

3 TO 4 ANCHOVY FILLETS

FRESHLY GROUND BLACK PEPPER

¼ CUP OLIVE OIL

2 TABLESPOONS GOOD VINEGAR, ANY VARIETY

Ruth was editor in chief of *Gourmet* for ten years, so we'll let her speak for herself.

She writes, "Puntarelle is a funny looking vegetable. When you peel away the long dark-green strands, what you find is a heart made up of little bulbs that look like fat, stubby white asparagus spears. Cut them off and cut them open, and you'll find that they're hollow inside. This is the part that Romans eat in the springtime. They cut the bulbs into long, thin strips and put them in ice water for an hour, until the strips curl. Although puntarelle has the reputation of being very bitter, the bulbs are not; it's the leaves that are."

Cut the puntarelle bulbs into long, thin strips and put them in ice water for an hour, until the strips curl.

Meanwhile make the anchovy sauce: Mash the garlic with a mortar and pestle until it pretty much disappears. Add the anchovy fillets and mash until they are reduced to a mushy paste. Grate in a good amount of pepper, then slowly add the olive oil and then vinegar until it is a powerful dressing that is to your taste.

Drain the puntarelle strips, transfer to a bowl, and toss them with the sauce.

TWO OTHER WONDERFUL WAYS
TO PREPARE PUNTARELLE

Sauteed Puntarelle Leaves

Remove the long, green leaves from a head of puntarelle. Blanch quickly in boiling salted water. Sauté in olive oil and garlic for 10 minutes, add salt and pepper to taste, and serve with a grating of Romano cheese and a dusting of crisp breadcrumbs.

Puntarelle à la Cinese

Slice the puntarelle bulbs into strips in the classic manner, but do not put into ice water.

Heat a wok and slick it with peanut or grapeseed oil. Throw in a couple of cloves of smashed garlic and an equal amount of diced ginger. Stir quickly, then add a handful of sliced shiitake mushrooms and stir for a few minutes, until the mushrooms are limp. Add the puntarelle and toss. Add a bit of chicken stock, and cook, tossing, just until the puntarelle wilts. Add a splash of soy sauce and a couple of tablespoons of oyster sauce and serve.

Farmer TRINA PILONERO
SILVER HEIGHTS FARM

Farmers market fare is often hailed as "slow food," and Trina Pilonero's wares just might be the slowest around. That's not only because she grows more than one thousand heirloom herb and vegetable varieties so staggeringly diverse that she represented Greenmarket at the Slow Food meeting in Italy in 2006. But it's also because the items she sells on the west side of Union Square are, quite literally, slow. Purchases at her stand won't be eaten for weeks or even months.

That's because Trina sells seedlings. A few dollars will afford you some fledgling fennel, inch-tall pea plants, and newly sprouted red scallions hardly thicker than hairs. In return for a tiny investment in time and attention, eaters willing to grow their own will reap seriously special produce as well as the invaluable experience of watching sunlight and soil yield your eventual dinner. It's delayed gratification, but flavor favors the patient.

Sure, scores of Greenmarket farmers sell seedlings each spring. But Trina has spent twenty-five years working to revive and promote varieties that you never see at the supermarket, and are even little known at farm stands. A banner at the back of her tent advertises "FUNKY ORGANIC HERBS," and her seedling catalog features breathtaking biodiversity, from three dozen kinds of cucumbers to three *hundred* types of tomatoes, all sprouted in her Catskills greenhouse and sold in seedling form. She can tell you the history of each and every one, whether it hails from Hungary or Hawaii, and specializes in species that are often very old, sometimes very rare, and always

◄ *Seed-saver Trina has spent twenty-five years reviving rare varieties. Her seedlings include three dozen kinds of cucumbers and three hundred types of tomatoes.* (Amanda Gentile)

open-pollinated—that's botany-speak for plants whose seeds, unlike those of commercial hybrid varieties beloved by industrial agriculture, reproduce "true to type" and thus can be saved and replanted for generations.

Although Silver Heights is based in Sullivan County, silver-haired Trina has curated a lineup uniquely suited to city life. While she steers New Yorkers with only airshaft light away from tomatoes and peppers, she's found many heirlooms that are perfectly happy in a sunny skyscraper or south-facing studio, like dwarf peas and tabletop lettuce planters. Some new New Yorkers, transplanted here from other countries, request her help finding varieties unknown stateside, sometimes bringing her seeds to coax into crops that taste like home.

> *In return for a tiny investment in time and attention, eaters willing to grow their own will reap seriously special produce.*

Although selling seedlings is her livelihood, Trina gladly shares her would-be trade secrets, teaching anyone the millennia-old practice of seed saving. Her catalog includes complete instruction on harvesting your own seeds, and she's led seed-saving workshops for urban gardeners through GrowNYC's Open Space Greening program, empowering her best customers to cut her out of the process. It might be counter to her business interests, but after decades spent sprouting seeds, Trina's ultimate objectives are in the soil of culture: planting ideas and cultivating agricultural knowledge wherever it can take root.

SUGAR SNAP PEA AND WHIPPED-RICOTTA TARTINES

by **DANA COWIN, EDITOR IN CHIEF, *FOOD & WINE***

Spring brings three kinds of peas—shell, snow, and snap. The first, as the name implies, must be shelled, but the other two have sweet, crunchy pods which the French call *mange tout*, meaning "eat it all."

But "eat it all" can have an even broader pea meaning: The plant's tender shoots are also perfectly edible, raw or cooked, and carry the true flavor of peas.

Here the pods and plants are served together, along with radishes, atop a tartine—or French open-faced sandwich—that's at once creamy and light, rustic and elegant.

1 CUP FRESH RICOTTA CHEESE

¼ CUP EXTRA VIRGIN OLIVE OIL, DIVIDED, PLUS MORE FOR BRUSHING

KOSHER SALT AND FRESHLY GROUND BLACK PEPPER

FOUR ½-INCH-THICK SLICES OF PEASANT BREAD

1 PEELED GARLIC CLOVE

½ POUND SUGAR SNAP PEAS, ENDS TRIMMED AND STRINGS DISCARDED

2½ TABLESPOONS CHAMPAGNE VINEGAR

1 TABLESPOON MINCED SHALLOT

2 TEASPOONS DIJON MUSTARD

½ CUP SNIPPED PEA SHOOTS

3 LARGE RADISHES, CUT INTO THIN MATCHSTICKS, ABOUT ⅓ CUP

CRUSHED RED PEPPER, FOR GARNISH

In a medium bowl, using a whisk, whip the ricotta with 2 tablespoons of olive oil and season with salt and pepper.

Preheat a grill pan. Brush the bread on both sides with olive oil. Grill over moderate heat, turning once, until toasted but still chewy in the middle, about 2 minutes. Rub the toasts with the garlic clove and season with salt and pepper.

Prepare an ice water bath. In a large saucepan of salted boiling water, blanch the snap peas until bright green, about 1 minute. Transfer the snap peas to the ice bath to cool. Drain and pat dry, then thinly slice lengthwise.

In a medium bowl, whisk the vinegar with the shallot, mustard, and the remaining 2 tablespoons of olive oil. Add the snap peas, pea shoots, and radishes; season with salt and pepper; and toss to coat. Spread the whipped ricotta on the toasts and top with the snap pea slaw. Garnish with crushed red pepper and serve.

MAKES 4 TARTINES

SQUID WITH WATERCRESS SALSA VERDE

by **CHESTER GERL, HUNDRED ACRES**

Potatoes

1 POUND YUKON GOLD POTATOES

2 TABLESPOONS OLIVE OIL

Salsa Verde

1 BUNCH WATERCRESS, ABOUT
3 OUNCES, ANY TOUGH STEMS
REMOVED

½ BUNCH FLAT-LEAF PARSLEY,
WITH STEMS

1 THINLY SLICED GARLIC CLOVE

ZEST AND JUICE OF ONE LEMON,
DIVIDED

PINCH RED CHILI FLAKES

1 ANCHOVY

½ TEASPOON SALT

1 TABLESPOON RED WINE VINEGAR

¼ CUP VEGETABLE OIL

2 TABLESPOONS OLIVE OIL

Squid

1¼ POUND SQUID, CLEANED

1 TABLESPOON OLIVE OIL

2 GARLIC CLOVES, CUT INTO
SLIVERS

½ TEASPOON ALEPPO PEPPER
(OPTIONAL)

½ TEASPOON SMOKED PAPRIKA

SALT TO TASTE

Squid deserves a spotlight. While many seafood choices come with warnings of mercury or overfishing, squid populations remain both clean and robust. Plus it's one of the most affordable proteins around and cooks in about a minute flat. Have your garlic prepped before you put the squid in the pan—it can go from tender to rubbery in a flash.

Watercress, as the name implies, likes its feet wet. Some Catskills farmers forage for the weed along the banks of pristine mountain streams, bringing the peppery plant to market by the bunch. Here watercress is whirred into a quick salsa verde you'll want to eat by the spoon. To make this dish an appetizer instead of an entrée, omit the potatoes.

Preheat the oven to 350°F.

Prepare the potatoes: In a large stockpot, cover whole potatoes with cold water. Salt generously and bring to a boil, reduce heat, and simmer for 20 to 25 minutes, or until the potatoes are fork tender. Drain, cool, and quarter the potatoes and place them on a sheet tray. Toss with the olive oil and salt. Bake for 15 minutes, or until light golden brown.

Make the salsa verde: In a food processor, combine the watercress, parsley, garlic, the lemon zest, 1 tablespoon lemon juice, chili flakes, anchovy, salt, and vinegar. With the motor running, drizzle in the oils. Season with additional salt and pepper to taste. Set aside.

Prepare the squid: Cut the squid into bite-size pieces. Heat a large sauté pan over medium-high heat. Once very hot, add the olive oil. Sauté the garlic for about 10 seconds, then add the squid and a pinch of salt. Toss and cook until opaque yet still tender, about 1 minute. Add the Aleppo and smoked paprika and sauté for 10 seconds. Add 1 tablespoon lemon juice and remove from the heat.

Toss the warm potatoes with a few spoonfuls of salsa verde. Top with the squid and pan juices and serve with additional salsa verde on the side.

SERVES 4

ORECCHIETTE WITH LAMB SAUSAGE AND BROCCOLI RABE

by **SAUL BOLTON, RESTAURANT SAUL, THE VANDERBILT, RED GRAVY**

Lamb Sausage

9 CLOVES GARLIC

1 MEDIUM SHALLOT

1 TABLESPOON OLIVE OIL

1 POUND GROUND LAMB

1 TEASPOON LEMON ZEST

1 TABLESPOON FRESH THYME LEAVES

¼ TEASPOON CHILI FLAKES

½ TEASPOON SALT

Pasta

1 SMALL BUNCH BROCCOLI RABE

12 OUNCES ORECCHIETTE PASTA

2 LARGE CIPOLLINI ONIONS

2 TABLESPOONS FRESH MINT

1 TABLESPOON EXTRA VIRGIN OLIVE OIL

½ CUP WHITE WINE

1 THINLY SLICED GARLIC CLOVE

PINCH OF RED CHILI FLAKES

½ CUP FINELY GRATED PECORINO

4 OUNCES SHEEP'S MILK FETA

Saul Bolton is a founding father of the Brooklyn food phenomenon, having landed the first Michelin star in that borough. But when 3-Corner Field Farm's Karen Weinberg called to congratulate him, Saul quickly replied that the award really belonged to farmers like her, on whose shoulders his flavors stand.

In this pasta, Saul honors both sides of Karen's sheep dairy, cooking up a simple DIY sausage from her ground lamb and finishing the dish with a shower of her grated feta. (Sure, you could easily prepare this with pre-made sausage, but Saul shows it's simple to season your own. You don't even need casings.)

The other star ingredient here is barely bitter broccoli rabe, one of the first green ingredients to appear at market each year. A good month before the tender young rabe, grown from new seeds, pops up from the soil, some farmers harvest "overwintered" rabe, rendered succulent and sweet by the cold months beneath the snow.

Make the sausage: Finely chop the garlic and shallot. In a small sauté pan, heat the olive oil over medium-low heat. Add the garlic, shallots, and a pinch of salt and cook until the shallots are translucent and sweet, 3 to 4 minutes. Transfer to a mixing bowl and let cool, then add the ground lamb, lemon zest, thyme, chili flakes, and salt and mix well to combine. Refrigerate until ready to use, up to two days.

Prepare the pasta: Peel any thick broccoli rabe stems and cut into 1-inch pieces, keeping florets and leaves separate. Bring a large pot of water to a boil and season well with salt. Blanch the stems for a minute, then add the florets; cook for an additional 30 seconds then remove with a slotted spoon and set aside. Add the pasta to the water and cook according to the manufacturer's instructions. Reserve ½ cup of the pasta water. Drain the pasta and keep warm in a large bowl.

Meanwhile thinly slice the onions, roughly chop the mint, and heat a large sauté pan over medium-high heat. Add the olive oil and the lamb sausage mixture in an even layer. Sear for 3 to 4 minutes, until the underside is golden brown. With a wooden spoon, break the sausage into small pieces. Add the cipollini and garlic and cook 3 minutes. Deglaze the pan with the wine and cook 2 more minutes. Add the broccoli rabe (raw leaves, and blanched stems and florets), then transfer the lamb mixture to the pasta bowl, add the chili flakes, Pecorino, and mint and toss to combine. If the pasta is too dry, add some reserved pasta water. Finish with an extra drizzle of olive oil and top with crumbled feta.

SERVES 4

SHALLOT

GREEN
GARLIC

CHIVE

GARLIC SCAPE

SHALLOT

RAMP

CIPOLLINI ONION

PURPLE CIPOLLINI
ONION

SCALLION

BUTTER-BRAISED MORELS WITH NETTLE PESTO AND LOCAL POLENTA

by **MARC MEYER, COOKSHOP**

People have hunted morel mushrooms each spring for thousands of years—and once you taste them, you'll know why. The distinctive honeycomb cap, which pokes up from the carpet of old leaves on the forest floor, holds a unique flavor that's a little earthy, a little tangy, and widely prized. Be sure to use a sauté pan large enough to fit them all in a single layer, or if necessary, cook them in batches.

Foraged stinging nettles also arrive at the market in early spring. As the name implies, the plant's tiny prickles can hurt your skin, so use gloves when handling it raw, or if the stems are young and tender, simply tip the bag's contents directly into the pot. Once cooked, the greens are toothless—and delicious.

Don't toss out the cooking water—many people seek out nettles precisely to make tea, for both its woodsy flavor and healthful properties.

Served atop polenta, this is a hearty, starchy comfort dish for a cold spring day.

Prepare the morels: In a large sauté pan, melt the butter over medium heat and allow it to foam. Add the shallots and cook for 4 minutes. Add the thyme, then the morels and stir. Reduce heat, cover, and cook for 15 minutes. Remove the lid and season with salt and pepper to taste, and set aside.

Make the polenta: Bring 2 cups of water to a boil in a heavy-bottom saucepot. Add 1 teaspoon of salt. Rapidly whisk in the polenta, then reduce heat to low and cook for 45 minutes, stirring occasionally. Remove from heat and stir in the cream and Parmesan. Adjust seasoning with salt and pepper, and set aside.

Morels

2 TABLESPOONS UNSALTED BUTTER

2 TABLESPOONS FINELY MINCED SHALLOTS

½ TEASPOON FRESH THYME LEAVES

½ POUND TRIMMED MOREL MUSHROOMS

SALT AND PEPPER

Polenta

½ CUP POLENTA

¼ CUP HEAVY CREAM

½ CUP GRATED PARMESAN

SALT AND FRESHLY GROUND BLACK PEPPER

Nettle Pesto

½ POUND NETTLES

1 MASHED GARLIC CLOVE

½ CUP WALNUTS

ZEST AND JUICE OF 1 LEMON

½ TEASPOON SALT

¾ CUP OLIVE OIL, DIVIDED

(continued) ▶

Prepare the nettle pesto: Fill a small stockpot with water, salt lightly, and bring to a boil. Wearing gloves, discard any tough stems from the nettles. Cook the greens in the boiling water for 2 minutes. Strain (see headnote) and rinse well under cold water. Press to remove as much water as possible.

In a food processor, combine the cooked nettles, garlic, walnuts, lemon zest, salt, and ¼ cup of olive oil. Pulse to a coarse, granular consistency, then, with the water running, add the remaining ½ cup of olive oil in a slow, even stream until you have a coarse, creamy paste. Do not overprocess.

Preheat the oven to 350°F.

Spread the polenta in a shallow baking dish and top with the morels. Heat in the oven for 15 minutes. Just before serving, add the lemon juice to the nettle pesto, adjust the salt to taste and serve over the warm polenta and morels.

SERVES 4

FRESH FETTUCCINE WITH SPRING GREENS

by **DAVID WALTUCK, EXECUTIVE CHEF, ARK RESTAURANTS**

Refined, market-driven menus made Chef Waltuck's Chanterelle one of the most revered restaurants in New York for more than thirty years, but this dish is easy enough to toss together on a busy weeknight. Just blanch a mix of early spring leaves—anything from young, tender dandelion to ramp tops to simple spinach. Green garlic also works well if it's young enough to resemble a scallion (though later in spring, as it grows taller and the bulb swells, it'll be too tough for this pesto-like preparation).

2 POUNDS MIXED SPRING GREENS, SUCH AS DANDELION, RAMPS, STINGING NETTLES, SPINACH, AND LAMB'S QUARTERS

1½ CUPS GRATED PARMESAN

¾ CUP PLUS 1 TABLESPOON EXTRA VIRGIN OLIVE OIL, DIVIDED

SALT AND PEPPER

ZEST AND JUICE OF 2 LEMONS, ABOUT 2 TEASPOONS ZEST AND 4 TABLESPOONS JUICE

1 POUND FRESH FETTUCCINE

1 CUP HEAVY CREAM

Bring a large pot of water, seasoned generously with salt, to a boil. Meanwhile, trim and wash the greens. If using ramps, separate the bulbs and save for another use such as pickled ramps on page 20. If using spinach or dandelion greens, remove any tough stems. If using stinging nettles, handle them with gloves while raw.

Add the greens to the pot of boiling water and blanch for 30 seconds to 1 minute, or until just wilted. Reserve the cooking water but remove the greens with a slotted spoon, transfer to a colander, and cool under cold running water. Squeeze to drain any liquid. You should have about 2 cups of cooked greens.

Transfer the cooked greens to a food processor and puree with the Parmesan, ¾ cup olive oil, ½ teaspoon salt, and zest and juice of the lemons, to a fairly smooth paste that still has some texture.

Return the pot of water to a boil, add the fettuccine and cook until al dente, about 2 to 3 minutes for fresh pasta. Reserve ⅓ cup of the pasta water, then drain the pasta well and return to the pot. Add the cream and pureed greens and toss gently to combine, thinning with the reserved pasta water as needed. Cook over low heat about 1 minute until the sauce just coats the pasta. Season with salt and pepper to taste, and serve with more Parmesan on the side.

SERVES 4

MOROCCAN GOAT CHOPS WITH SPRING SALAD

by **ANTHONY SASSO, CASA MONO**

Marinade

1 TEASPOON GROUND CORIANDER

1 TEASPOON GROUND CUMIN

1 TEASPOON GROUND PAPRIKA

1 TEASPOON GROUND CINNAMON

1 TEASPOON DRIED MINT
(OPTIONAL)

2 FINELY CHOPPED GARLIC CLOVES

¼ CUP VEGETABLE OIL

1 TEASPOON SALT

8 BONE-IN GOAT CHOPS, ABOUT
2½ POUNDS TOTAL

Salad

¼ CUP OLIVE OIL

1 TEASPOON HONEY

2 TABLESPOONS WHITE WINE
VINEGAR

1 TABLESPOON LEMON JUICE

8 THINLY SLICED PICKLED RAMP
BOTTOMS (PAGE 20, OPTIONAL)

1 POUND ASPARAGUS, WOODY
BOTTOMS SNAPPED OFF

6 ENGLISH BREAKFAST RADISHES

2 CUPS PEA GREENS

4 OUNCES FRESH GOAT CHEESE

¼ CUP ROUGHLY CHOPPED MINT

SALT AND FRESHLY GROUND
BLACK PEPPER

It's hard to believe that just a few decades ago, goat cheese was altogether unheard of in America. But chèvre has gained a sure footing on our shores, and today goat milk, cheese, and yogurt are found in farmers markets and even mainstream supermarkets nationwide. Goat meat, on the other hand, remains uncommon in American cuisine.

Before a nanny can be milked, she has to have a kid or two, and while her daughters can grow up to be dairy goats too, the young rams' only culinary destiny is a knife and fork. Which means farmers selling goat cheese often have a cooler full of delicious meat.

Goat chops are very similar to lamb, and a snap to cook—just two minutes per side and you're done. Here Chef Sasso gives them a Moroccan rub and serves them alongside a fresh salad of raw asparagus, radishes, and mint with—what else?—goat cheese.

Marinate the chops: In a small bowl whisk together the marinade ingredients, then pour over the goat chops (a pie plate works well for this) and refrigerate, covered, for 4 to 6 hours.

Make the vinaigrette: In another small bowl, whisk together the olive oil, honey, white wine vinegar, lemon juice, and pickled ramps, if using. Season with salt to taste and set aside.

Prepare the salad: Using a mandolin or a sharp knife, slice the asparagus spears on the bias, about ⅛-inch thick. Thinly slice the radishes, also to about ⅛-inch, and reserve the leaves. Combine the asparagus, radishes, pea greens, crumbled goat cheese, and mint in a bowl. Season with salt and pepper and set aside.

To cook the goat chops: Set a cast-iron skillet over medium-high heat. Remove the chops from the marinade, without being too fussy about scraping off the spices, and season with salt on each side. Once the pan is very hot, add 1 tablespoon of olive oil. Working in two batches so as not to crowd the pan, sear the first four chops for about 2 minutes, then turn and cook the other side for an additional 2 minutes. Transfer to a plate to rest. Wipe out the oil from the pan, and add 1 tablespoon of olive oil and cook the second batch of chops.

In the same warm pan, quickly wilt the reserved radish tops, 30 seconds to 1 minute, and then add them to the salad and dress with the vinaigrette just before serving. Serve two chops per plate with the salad alongside.

SERVES 4

BLACK SEA BASS WITH RAINBOW
AND DELFINO CILANTRO

IL BUCO

2 LARGE CARROTS

1 RIB CELERY

ONE ½-INCH PIECE GINGER
(ABOUT THE DIAMETER OF
A QUARTER)

1 CUP CARROT JUICE, FROM ABOUT
4 LARGE CARROTS, PEELED

SALT

PINCH CAYENNE PEPPER

1 BUNCH RAINBOW CARROTS,
ABOUT 8 TO 10 CARROTS

3 TABLESPOONS GOOD EXTRA
VIRGIN OLIVE OIL

1½ LIMES

A FEW LARGE LETTUCE LEAVES

4 (6-OUNCE) FILLETS BLACK
SEA BASS

1 BUNCH DELFINO CILANTRO

Black sea bass has an edible skin with pretty black hatching that evokes herringbone and a white flesh that cooks up tender and sweet. The fish (which isn't really a bass) can be baked, seared, or poached in minutes. Here fillets are steamed, quickly and cleanly, over lettuce leaves, then served atop a wonderfully light carrot puree. You can, of course, stick with orange carrots, but farmers such as Paffenroth Gardens' Alex Paffenroth lure chefs with a spectrum from off-white to burgundy.

Peel the two large carrots and slice crosswise about ½-inch thick. Peel the ginger and slice it and the celery into pieces of the same size.

In a medium saucepot combine ½ cup of the carrot juice, the sliced carrots, celery, and ginger, and a pinch of salt and cayenne and bring to a simmer, covered, over medium heat. The juice will not cover the vegetables so you will have to stir them occasionally to ensure they cook evenly. Simmer for about 10 minutes, or until a fork can easily pierce the vegetables.

Meanwhile, prepare a bowl of ice water, scrub the rainbow carrots well and trim the green tops 2 inches above the root. With a mandolin, shave the carrots thinly lengthwise. Place the shaved carrots into the ice water and rest for 15 minutes.

In a blender, combine the cooked carrot-celery mixture with the remaining ½ cup of carrot juice. Puree on high for 2 minutes, until smooth. (If the mixture is too thick, add additional carrot juice or water, 1 tablespoon at a time, to thin so that it can puree). With the blender on low, drizzle in the olive oil and finish with the juice of ½ lime. Chill. Season to taste with salt.

In a large stockpot, prepare a steamer basket over an inch of water over high heat. Bring to a simmer, reduce heat to medium, line the steamer basket with the lettuce leaves, and lay the bass fillets on the leaves. Steam the fish, covered, for 2 to 3 minutes or until just cooked through.

Meanwhile, remove the shaved carrots from the ice water and dry on a towel. Transfer to a mixing bowl and add the juice of the remaining lime and a pinch of salt. Gently mix by hand.

Set out four plates and spoon ½ cup of the chilled carrot puree onto each. Place the bass across the puree and arrange the shaved carrots over and around the bass. Finish with a drizzle of good extra virgin olive oil, sea salt, and small leaves of the Delfino cilantro.

SERVES 4

SORREL AND GOAT CHEESE QUICHE

by **AMY HESS, NORTHERN SPY FOOD CO.**

Crust

1½ CUPS ALL-PURPOSE FLOUR

1 TEASPOON SALT

4 OUNCES (1 STICK) UNSALTED BUTTER, COLD AND DICED INTO ½-INCH CUBES

5 TABLESPOONS ICE COLD WATER (STRAIN ICE BEFORE USING)

Egg mixture

6 LARGE EGGS

1½ CUPS HEAVY CREAM

¾ TEASPOON SALT

⅛ TEASPOON GROUND NUTMEG

Sorrel filling

1 TABLESPOON UNSALTED BUTTER

1 POUND SORREL, FROM ABOUT 2 BUNCHES, TOUGH STEMS DISCARDED

8 OUNCES SOFT GOAT CHEESE, AT ROOM TEMPERATURE

½ TEASPOON LEMON ZEST, FROM ABOUT ½ LEMON

¾ TEASPOON SALT

¼ TEASPOON FRESHLY GROUND BLACK PEPPER

1 TABLESPOON DIJON MUSTARD (OPTIONAL)

When the market bursts to life with young green things each spring, be sure to seek out sorrel. Also called sourgrass, the plant is high in oxalic acid, which gives both the stems and leaves a wonderful citrusy brightness, accentuated here by the acidity of lemon zest and Dijon. Don't worry about texture when cooking the sorrel—it can seem a little slimy in the pan, but once it bakes, it's similar to spinach, albeit with that signature tang.

This quiche can be served warm, at room temperature, or cold. It makes a beautiful lunch or light dinner alongside a fresh green salad, or pack it for a picnic on a warm spring day.

Prepare the crust: In the bowl of a stand mixer fitted with the paddle attachment, combine the flour, salt, and butter and mix on low speed until the mixture resembles coarse meal. With the mixer still running, slowly add ice water until the mixture just starts to come together. Turn the dough onto a lightly floured surface and without overworking, shape into a disk. Wrap in plastic and chill for 1 hour or overnight.

When ready to bake, preheat the oven to 375°F.

Roll the dough out on a lightly floured surface to a ¼-inch thickness and fit into a 9-inch pie tin or quiche pan. Using parchment paper and pie weights, blind bake the shell for 30 minutes. Remove the weights and parchment paper and bake for 5 more minutes. Remove from the oven and cool to room temperature.

Make the egg mixture: Whisk the eggs, heavy cream, salt, and nutmeg in a medium mixing bowl and set aside.

Prepare the sorrel filling: Heat a large skillet over medium heat. Melt the butter, then add the sorrel. Cook until the sorrel is wilted and the liquid is evaporated, about 3 minutes. Transfer the sorrel to a plate lined with paper towels to dry further.

In a mixing bowl, use a rubber spatula to combine the goat cheese with the lemon zest, salt, pepper.

To prepare quiche for baking: Prepare the oven to 425°F.

Brush the bottom of the crust with Dijon mustard, if using. Next, spread the goat cheese mixture onto the crust in an even layer. Place the cooled sorrel atop the goat cheese. Lastly, pour the egg mixture to about ¼-inch below the top of the crust.

Bake for 15 minutes, then turn the oven down to 350°F and bake for another 15 to 20 minutes or until the quiche is set.

MAKES 1 9-INCH QUICHE

Farmer FRANCA TANTILLO
BERRIED TREASURES FARM

If the movie *Working Girl* had been about breaking the glass ceiling in agriculture instead of investment banking, the final scene would have shown Melanie Griffith selling strawberries to an awestruck chef David Bouley—played, of course, by Harrison Ford.

In other words, it would have shown the real-life success of Franca Tantillo.

Franca Tantillo is a Staten Island native with the accent to prove it, but the specialty ingredients she brings to market—from stinging nettles and *haricot verts* to adulation-inspiring strawberries—lure chefs like a siren song. She passes all the credit to her soil. "It's the mineral that matters," she tells anyone who will listen. "That's what it's all about."

City raised and trained as a nurse, Franca says farming was in her genes—her father had farmed in Sicily before immigrating to America, and as with all the Italian immigrants in her neighborhood, he tended a big garden out back.

By her early twenties, Franca was working with drug and alcohol detox patients on St. Vincent's "hall from hell" when a car accident left her with two broken vertebrae. Doctors were pushing Valium; instead she moved up to the Catskills to heal herself.

She soon became nurse to Dr. Carey Reams, an alternative medicine proponent who correlated illness to mineral deficiencies, used a refractometer to measure sugar content in vegetables, and believed enriched soil was the foundation of human health. One of his mottos was, "Farmers are the best doctors in the world."

◄ *Franca says her secret is her soil. "The higher the minerals,"* *she repeats, "the sweeter the plant."* (Amanda Gentile)

"And that," says Franca, "is why all day long my customers say, 'WOW.'"

Soon Franca and her husband started their own farm, practicing what Reams had preached. A friend in Brooklyn called and said, "You kids should try this thing called the Greenmarket!" One divorce later, she renamed the property Berried Treasures; 1994 was her first season on her own.

Franca threw herself into the work, harvesting at night with a headlamp, foraging wild watercress along mountain streams, and making jams and jellies until 2 in the morning. But most of all, she tended to her soil, enriching it each year with thousands of pounds of chicken manure, green sand, cotton, mineral powders, and, most importantly, calcium phosphate, which she says acts like sunshine, allowing each plant to pull in all the other minerals.

"The higher the minerals," she repeats like a mantra, "the sweeter the plant. Your God-given gift is your tongue. If it's sweet," and she's not just talking about fruit here, "that's what you should be buying."

But Franca doesn't only measure minerals with her mouth. She carries a refractometer, the tool Dr. Reams swore by. (It's also as common as a corkscrew on vineyards, where grape growers and wine makers test sugar content, knowing, say, the precise moment to harvest.) Simply add a few drops of any liquid, whether squeezed from champagne grapes or Franca's peas, and it gives you a number. The sweeter the juice, the higher the number.

Franca swears by the natural sugars healthy plants carry in high levels. "You're searching for a pharmaceutical company to mask symptoms," she explains, channeling her nurse days, "but if you give your body the right elements, it will heal itself."

Chefs prescribe their customers high doses of Franca's crops for another reason—pure flavor. Her cold climate may delay her harvests—her English shelling peas don't come in until most other farmers are already done—but the taste makes them well worth the wait. She's most famous for her tiny day-neutral "Tristar" strawberries. Crossed with a mountain variety and retaining all fifty-one aromatic compounds of the wild kind, Tristars were developed by two PhDs whom Franca regards as candidates for canonization. "They should have a claim to fame in heaven," she laughs. "I'll see them up there."

But despite her mastery of seeds and soil, she's just as well known for ingredients she didn't grow at all—the ones she forages up in the mountains. Watercress, fiddleheads, lambs quarters, and stinging nettle in spring, then day lily buds, sumac, elderberries, wild blueberries, and wild apples as the months go by. The most famous of these is also the first—ramps. This wild allium, which looks something like its domestic cousins scallions and leeks, appears overnight on mountainsides and then menus each May.

Franca's long list of chef clients include Michael Romano, David Bouley, Daniel Boulud, Andrew Carmellini, Jean-Georges Vongerichten, Ignacio Mattos, April Bloomfield, and the many sous chefs who once cooked in these kitchens and now command their own, from Blue Hill to startups in Brooklyn. But not everyone shopping at her stand runs a restaurant—not by a long shot.

"It's still my pleasure to feed and heal people," she says. "That's what gives me the drive. Yesterday I got little kids to taste my tomatoes. When you see those shining little eyes, it makes it all worth it. And those are the people I try to tell—it's the minerals that matter."

PAVLOVA WITH STRAWBERRIES AND BASIL

by **MARTHA STEWART, MARTHA STEWART LIVING OMNIMEDIA**

This meringue miracle is a snap to whip up, and the result is an absolute showstopper, perfect for Easter or Passover. Simply beat egg whites with a few pantry staples until soft peaks form, spread onto a cookie sheet, and bake. The resulting confection is gorgeous, delicious, and light as air—which is why it was named after the Russian ballerina Anna Pavlova. When ready to serve, top it with whipped cream and strawberries, or as spring turns to summer, whatever fruit is ripe for the picking. The berry-basil flavors marry well, or garnish with edible violets.

Preheat the oven to 300°F with a rack in the center. Line a baking sheet with parchment paper.

Make the meringue base: Place the egg whites, salt, and brown sugar in the bowl of an electric mixer fitted with the whisk attachment. Beat on low speed until no lumps of sugar remain. Increase the speed to medium; beat until soft peaks form, about 9 minutes. With the mixer running, gradually add the superfine sugar. Continue beating until peaks are stiff and glossy, about 2 minutes more. Beat in the vinegar and vanilla.

Using a rubber spatula, spread the meringue into an 8-inch circle on the baking sheet; form peaks around the edge and a well in the center.

Bake until crisp around the edge and just set in the center, about 1¼ hours. Transfer to a wire rack until cool enough to handle. Carefully peel off the parchment, and let the meringue cool completely on the rack.

Make the topping: Slice the strawberries lengthwise, about ¼-inch thick. Toss with the granulated sugar and let sit to macerate for 10 to 15 minutes, stirring occasionally.

Just before serving, whip the heavy cream and vanilla until soft peaks form. Place the meringue on a serving platter and top with whipped cream and strawberries and juices, and garnish with basil.

SERVES 6

Meringue Base

Meringue Base

- **4 LARGE EGG WHITES**
- **PINCH OF SALT**
- **¾ CUP PACKED LIGHT BROWN SUGAR**
- **¼ CUP SUPERFINE SUGAR**
- **1 TEASPOON DISTILLED WHITE VINEGAR**
- **1 TEASPOON PURE VANILLA EXTRACT**

Topping

- **1 QUART STRAWBERRIES**
- **2 TABLESPOONS GRANULATED SUGAR**
- **¾ CUP HEAVY CREAM**
- **½ TEASPOON VANILLA**
- **2 TABLESPOONS SMALL BASIL LEAVES, LIGHTLY PACKED**

PICKLED STRAWBERRY JAM

by **CHRISTINA TOSI, MOMOFUKU MILK BAR**

1 TEASPOON SALT

1¾ CUPS SUGAR

1 TABLESPOON PECTIN

2 TABLESPOONS SHERRY VINEGAR

1 TABLESPOON RICE WINE VINEGAR

1 PIECE CARDAMOM

5 PIECES CORIANDER

3 CUPS STRAWBERRIES, HULLED AND QUARTERED

Christina Tosi is famous for her super-sweet (and salty), over-the-top confection inventions such as the compost cookie, "cereal milk" soft serve, and crack pie. But while her riff on strawberry jam contains salt, spices, and two kinds of vinegar, its flavor is surprisingly subtle, with extra acid giving it just a little boost of brightness. And while her jam is right at home on toast, Tosi also suggests slathering it on crêpes, swirling it into coffee cake batter, or mixing it up with equal parts softened butter for a killer spread on bread or biscuits.

If you prefer a less-seeded jam, just puree the berries in a blender and strain through a sieve before adding to the jam mixture. Overripe, bruised, or otherwise cosmetically imperfect fruit is perfect for preserving—if it tastes good, it doesn't matter what it looks like. And later in the season, come back to this recipe with the tiny "day-neutral" strawberries known as Tristars, a variety that was crossed with a wild berry and inherited its little size and big flavor.

In a small bowl, mix together the salt, sugar and pectin. Set aside.

In a medium pot over high heat, combine the vinegars with the cardamom and coriander. Bring just to a boil, then remove from heat and discard the spices. Return the pot to medium heat, sprinkle in the sugar mixture, and whisk to combine.

Whisk in the strawberries and bring to a boil, stirring occasionally. Turn the heat down to low and cook, stirring occasionally, for 3 minutes. The mixture will thicken. (You can mash the berries in the pot at this point to create a thicker, smoother jam.)

Pour the hot jam into a heat-safe bowl and cool completely. Store covered in the refrigerator or freeze.

MAKES 3 CUPS

LEMON THYME PANNA COTTA WITH RHUBARB COMPOTE AND LEMON THYME SHORTBREAD

by **PICHET ONG, PASTRY CHEF, BLOG.PICHETONG.COM**

You can make just one or two of this recipe's three components—they're wonderful alone or in any combination—but each part is so simple, it's easy to make them all. Pastry Chef Pichet Ong's yogurt panna cotta is sublime, requiring so little work, you'll want to make it all year long as a creamy canvas for whatever berries you bring home.

Lemon thyme, whose leaves have little yellow edges and a fragrant citrus flavor, is transformative on lemon-loving mains like scallops or roast chicken, but it's also bright and beautiful in sweets.

Variation inspiration: you can swap out the thyme for lavender, which is available May through July, for a flavor that's both fresh and floral.

Make the panna cotta: In a medium saucepan, combine the lemon thyme, milk, cream, sugar, and salt over medium heat and bring just to a simmer. Remove from heat, cover, and let steep at room temperature for about 1 hour. Remove and discard the thyme.

In a small bowl, combine the gelatin with 2 tablespoons of cold water. Stir to combine and let sit for 10 minutes. Meanwhile, return the milk mixture to a low simmer (do not boil) then add the gelatin mixture and stir well. As soon as the gelatin dissolves, remove from the heat. Whisk in the yogurt and divide into 8 glasses or 4-ounce ramekins. Refrigerate until set, at least 5 hours.

Meanwhile, make the compote: Combine all ingredients except the strawberries in a small saucepan and let sit for 20 minutes to macerate. Cook over low heat until the rhubarb is soft, about 7 minutes. Remove from heat and let cool. Once cool, add the sliced strawberries.

Panna Cotta

4 SPRIGS LEMON THYME

1 CUP MILK

1½ CUPS CREAM

1 CUP SUGAR

¼ TEASPOON SALT

1¾ TEASPOONS POWDERED GELATIN

1 CUP PLAIN WHOLE MILK YOGURT

Rhubarb-Strawberry Compote

3 TO 4 MEDIUM STALKS RHUBARB, TRIMMED AND CUT INTO ¼-INCH DICE (2 CUPS)

3 TABLESPOONS SUGAR

1 VANILLA BEAN, SPLIT, SCRAPED, AND HALVED CROSSWISE

1 TABLESPOON LEMON JUICE, FROM ABOUT ½ OF A LEMON

½ CUP SLICED STRAWBERRIES

(continued) ▶

Make the lemon thyme shortbread: Line a sheet pan with parchment paper and sprinkle lightly with sugar.

In a stand mixer with the paddle attachment, blend together the lemon thyme leaves, lemon zest, butter, sugar, vanilla, and salt just until thoroughly combined. Add the flour and mix until the dough comes together. Form the dough into a rectangle, about 1-inch thick, and cover with plastic wrap. Refrigerate until cold, about 1 hour.

On a lightly floured surface, roll the chilled dough into a large rectangle, about ½-inch thick.

Using a knife, cut rectangular cookies about 3½ inches long by 1 inch wide. Transfer cookies onto a parchment-lined cookie sheet, cover with plastic wrap, and refrigerate for 30 minutes.

Preheat the oven to 325°F.

Bake the chilled cookies until the edges turn golden brown, 15 to 18 minutes. Let cool on the cookie sheet for 2 minutes, then transfer to a wire rack to cool completely.

Garnish each panna cotta with 2 tablespoons of compote and serve alongside the shortbread.

SERVES 8

Lemon Thyme Shortbread

2 TABLESPOONS LEMON THYME LEAVES, PICKED FROM 1 SMALL BUNCH

ZEST OF 1 LEMON

11 TABLESPOONS UNSALTED BUTTER, AT ROOM TEMPERATURE

½ CUP SUGAR, PLUS MORE FOR SPRINKLING

1 TEASPOON VANILLA EXTRACT

¼ TEASPOON SALT

1 CUP PLUS 2 TABLESPOONS ALL-PURPOSE FLOUR

Farmer RONNY OSOFSKY
RONNYBROOK FARM DAIRY

In 1941, the year Ronny Osofsky was born, his parents founded a dairy farm and named it after him: Ronnybrook. Starting out, they did things the old fashioned way, even using horses to tend to the corn and hay that the cows would eat all winter. But agriculture was changing. When Ronny was a boy, his dad bought the farm's first tractor and let his little boy "steer."

"I thought I was driving," laughs Ronny, now seventy-two.

The family milked about a hundred cows and for decades, like just about every dairy farm in America—and the eighteen in their town alone—they sold their milk wholesale to processors who homogenized it with the outputs of hundreds of other herds before selling it to supermarkets. Each middleman took a cut, leaving little for the farmers.

In the 1980s, in addition to twice-daily milking, the Osofskys sold bulls to dairies in Europe, China, and Russia. One year, a creature named Ronnybrook Prelude was deemed the best bull in the world by dairy sire summaries. They'd sold him for about seven grand. The stud eventually went for $20 million.

But while some made hay on the global market, small farmers generally did not. Commodity prices were constantly swinging, and after the Stock Market crash of 1987, dairy farmers everywhere saw the bottom fall out. Suddenly the Osofskys couldn't even cover their operating costs.

"After the crash," recalls Ronny, "we knew we had to do something different to stay afloat." Assessing

◀ *After the crash of 1987, recalls Ronny, "we knew we had to do something different to stay afloat." Soon a proudly unhomogenized institution was born, literally the cream of the crop.* (Amanda Gentile)

their limited options, the family realized they had one thing many American farmers didn't: close proximity to New York City. So although Ronny had only been to Manhattan once or twice in his life, an idea soon rose to the top.

It was at once revolutionary and nothing new: great milk from one herd of grass-fed cows, bottled right on the farm in glass bottles, and sold directly to city customers who care about what's in their glass. In other words, the total opposite of the commodity market that had nearly milked small farmers dry.

The Osofskys didn't know of a single farmer bottling their own milk, but they sought out shuttered operations that had done so a generation or two before, buying a piece of old equipment in Massachusetts, another in New Hampshire. Ronny mortgaged the farm, borrowed money, got two grants, spent about a hundred thousand on infrastructure, and by the summer of 1991 was ready to launch. Ronnybrook's milk and cream debuted at the Greenmarket on July 4. Customers came out in droves, and a New York institution was founded.

Selling directly to customers meant the Osofskys now earned about three times what they'd been paid when selling their milk to a processor. But the farm also had "a lot more expenses," Ronny laughs. "That I found out!"

Bottom line, though, it was a huge success: The Osofskys were able to save the farm. Of the eighteen dairies in Pine Plains a few decades ago, only two are still in business today. (Ronnybrook's retail experiment didn't just save itself—the brand benefited a few others, because the Osofskys supplement their herd's supply with milk from three neighboring family farms, and now also custom bottle milk for two others.)

Today the Osofskys tend about 120 grass-fed milking cows, all the offspring of their long line of prize-winning Holsteins, plus three Jerseys to increase the butterfat—not for nothing is their milk called "Creamline." Pasteurized by law but proudly unhomogenized, each bottle bears a nice big cap of fat, literally the cream of the crop. The Culinary Institute of America can't get enough of the crème fraîche, and many city chefs cook with Ronnybrook butter, which clocks in around 87 percent butterfat (conventional butter has just 81 percent).

It was at once revolutionary and nothing new: great milk from grass-fed cows, bottled right on the farm in glass bottles, and sold directly to city customers who care about what's in their glass.

Ronnybrook won the blue ribbon in 2012 for best butter at the World Dairy Expo in Madison, Wisconsin. But Ronny says the Greenmarkets—they now sell at more than a dozen locations—remain the place where they get the most gratification.

"Greenmarket has been very instrumental in our growing," Ronny said. "But beyond the economics, there's a real satisfaction. People come to us every day and say that they've been shopping at our stand for twenty years and really appreciate what we're doing. That's very important to me."

Today Ronny's four children take care of the cows and markets, and his grandkids show calves at the fair. Ronny still steers when they harvest the hay, and he still drinks milk by the glass every day.

GREEN GIANT

by **TOM MACY, CLOVER CLUB**

4 SUGAR SNAP PEAS, PLUS 2 MORE
FOR GARNISH

8 TO 10 LEAVES TARRAGON

.75 OUNCE SIMPLE SYRUP
(EQUAL PARTS WATER AND
SUGAR SIMMERED UNTIL SUGAR
DISSOLVES, THEN CHILLED)

2 OUNCES HAYMAN'S OLD TOM GIN

.75 OUNCE LEMON JUICE

.5 OUNCE DRY VERMOUTH

When it comes to produce in cocktails, fruit has long hogged the lime-light. But recently, mixologists have devised ways to drink your vegetables, too. Clover Club's head barman Tom Macy was working on a menu of vegetal cocktails one spring when some sugar snap peas caught his eye. Muddling the whole, sweet pods carries their crisp flavor into the gin, and the tarragon is a match made in God's garden.

Old Tom Gin is an older style that is lighter and slightly sweeter than your typical London Dry Gin. Hayman's in particular really makes this cocktail soar. The drink is still great with London Dry Gin—just omit the dry vermouth.

Macy says the Green Giant epitomizes a great cocktail experience in that it's unique and yet completely approachable and delicious. The pretty garnish also makes everyone else at the bar want their own. "Whenever someone orders a Green Giant," he says, "I start prepping for a bunch."

Muddle the sugar snap peas and tarragon leaves in the simple syrup. Add the remaining ingredients, shake with ice, and strain into a rocks glass over crushed ice.

Garnish with two sugar snap peas.

MAKES 1 COCKTAIL

STRAWBERRY MINT JULEP

by **GABLE ERENZO, TUTHILLTOWN SPIRITS DISTILLERS**

New York State's first distillery since prohibition, Tuthilltown spins local corn and grains into liquid gold. Here their four-grain bourbon muddles up with mint into a strawberry-kissed julep that's dangerously easy to drink.

To crush a tray of ice, fill a Lewis bag, or just a clean pillow case, with cubes and smash them with a meat tenderizer or muddler. This drink just gets better as the ice melts. Raise a glass to spring.

Muddle the sugar, mint, and strawberries in a Julep cup or a Collins/highball glass. Fill the cup with crushed ice, add bourbon, and stir. Top off with more crushed ice and serve with a straw.

MAKES 1 COCKTAIL

1 TABLESPOON POWDERED SUGAR

8 TO 10 MINT LEAVES

3 MEDIUM-SIZE RIPE STRAWBERRIES

2½ OUNCES HUDSON FOUR GRAIN BOURBON

◂ The Hudson Valley was once the region's breadbasket. Today's grain-growing renaissance benefits artisan bakers and small-batch booze-makers.

Summer

CUCUMBER SOUP

by KENNETH WISS, DINER AND MARLOW & SONS

6 TO 7 CUCUMBERS, ABOUT
3½ POUNDS

⅓ CUP LIME JUICE, FROM ABOUT
3 LIMES

½ CUP OLIVE OIL, DIVIDED

¼ CUP LOOSELY PACKED
FRESH DILL LEAVES

¼ CUP LOOSELY PACKED
TARRAGON LEAVES

SALT AND FRESHLY GROUND
BLACK PEPPER

½ CUP LOOSELY PACKED
BASIL LEAVES

½ CUP LOOSELY PACKED
MINT LEAVES

Some Garnishes We've Loved

TOASTED ALMONDS

FRESH BLACKBERRIES

WATERMELON

CURRY YOGURT OR CRÈME
FRAÎCHE

ANY FRESH HERBS

In 1999 a tiny restaurant called Diner opened in Williamsburg, Brooklyn, proudly planting the farm-to-table flag in the nascent neighborhood. Fifteen years later, the kitchen at Diner is famous—and as honest and unpretentious as ever, with a steadfast commitment to local farmers, including those who set up each Saturday at the nearby McCarren Park Greenmarket.

Back in the day, that market's longtime manager, Ken Wiss, got to know the Diner crew when they shopped at the market each Saturday. Keen to learn about kitchens, Ken asked if he could come stage at their stoves. Soon Ken was working the line, and a decade later he's the restaurant's head chef. He still works closely with Greenmarket farmers—though now as their customer.

Ken's cucumber soup is fantastically refreshing—an herb-kissed variation on a classic summer dish he's served at Diner studded with everything from almonds to beets.

Peel the cucumbers and halve lengthwise. Using a spoon, scrape the seeds from half of the cucumbers, so the soup is not too bitter. Slice the cucumbers thinly and transfer to a large mixing bowl. Toss with the lime juice, ¼ cup of olive oil, dill, tarragon, 2 teaspoons of salt, and ½ teaspoon of black pepper. Dress the cucumbers like a salad that you would eat raw and let sit for one hour. The seasoning will marinate the cucumbers, and they will begin to break down and release liquid.

Transfer the mixture and its liquid to a blender (in batches if needed) and add the basil and mint. Blend at high speed, stopping to scrape down as needed. Puree for at least one minute, until perfectly smooth. Reduce the blender speed to medium-low and slowly drizzle in the remaining ¼ cup of olive oil. Adjust seasoning with salt, pepper, and lime juice and serve chilled.

SERVES 4 TO 6

CREAM OF EGGPLANT SOUP

by **KERRY HEFFERNAN, AUTHOR OF THE UPCOMING**
A YEAR ON THE EAST END: MY SEASONS IN SAG HARBOR

Most people think of eggplant as deep purple, but the ingredient was named for the white variety, which indeed resembles eggs. Peaking during late summer and early fall, it has an exceptionally soft texture and mild flavor. With the additional richness of butter, leeks, and cream, Chef Heffernan's soup is velvety and absolutely luscious. Marjoram—a sweeter cousin of oregano—adds a light piney-citrus note.

Served neat, this dish is a summer comfort, but here are some ideas to dress it up for company: Roast three red or yellow bell peppers, peel and julienne, then serve a few slices atop each bowl. Or slice an additional slender white eggplant into thin rounds, dredge in egg and breadcrumbs, and fry until golden and crisp.

12 SPRIGS MARJORAM, DIVIDED

2 SPRIGS EACH OF PARSLEY, TARRAGON, AND THYME

2 TABLESPOONS UNSALTED BUTTER

1 LEEK, WHITES ONLY, MINCED AND RINSED WELL

1 SMALL WHITE EGGPLANT, ABOUT 2 POUNDS, TRIMMED OF ANY STEM AND DICED, SKIN ON

2 FINELY MINCED GARLIC CLOVES

1 QUART GOOD CHICKEN STOCK

½ CUP HEAVY CREAM

1 TEASPOON WHITE WINE VINEGAR

SALT AND FRESHLY GROUND BLACK PEPPER

Tie four of the sprigs of marjoram into a bundle with the parsley, tarragon, and thyme. Set aside.

In a 6-quart, heavy-bottomed saucepot, melt the butter. Add the leeks and a pinch of salt and sweat gently for 2 to 3 minutes until the leeks soften. If the leeks begin to brown, add 1 tablespoon of water. Add the diced eggplant and the garlic, season well with salt and pepper and continue to cook for two minutes on medium heat, again ensuring that no browning occurs.

Add the bundle of herbs and chicken stock and simmer over medium-low heat for 15 to 18 minutes, or until the eggplant is tender. Add the cream, bring just to the boiling point, and remove immediately from the heat. Cover with a lid and let cool for 15 minutes.

Discard the bundle of herbs and transfer the pot's contents to a blender. Cover and carefully blend on high for 2 minutes or until very smooth, working in batches if needed. Add the vinegar, and adjust the seasoning for salt and pepper.

Finely chop the leaves of the remaining 8 sprigs of marjoram. Whisk into the soup to finish.

SERVES 4 TO 6

WARM SUMMER VEGETABLE SALAD

by **MARCO CANORA, HEARTH**

1 SMALL RED ONION, HALVED AND SLICED THINLY

½ GRATED GARLIC CLOVE

1 ANCHOVY FILLET, PULVERIZED TO PASTE

3 TABLESPOONS RED WINE VINEGAR

2 MEDIUM YUKON GOLD POTATOES, ABOUT ¾ POUND, PEELED AND QUARTERED

½ POUND MIXED BEANS, SUCH AS GREEN AND YELLOW ROMANO AND STRING BEANS, ENDS TRIMMED AND CUT IN HALF

1 SMALL ZUCCHINI, ABOUT 5 OUNCES, SLICED ¼-INCH THICK

¼ CUP EXTRA VIRGIN OLIVE OIL

3 TABLESPOONS ROUGHLY CHOPPED FRESH BASIL

SALT AND FRESHLY GROUND BLACK PEPPER

From across the kitchen, this dish may look like a salad at a church picnic. But take a bite and instead of the American Midwest, you'll taste Italy's *cucina povera*. The onion gets prettily pickled—toss it occasionally to keep it in the vinegar—while the anchovy gives the dish a subtle umami. This recipe easily doubles—and keeps beautifully—so go ahead and make a big batch.

Combine the onion, garlic, anchovy, and vinegar in the bottom of a large mixing bowl and set aside.

Bring a large pot of salted water to a boil. Add the potatoes and cook for 12 to 14 minutes, or until fork tender. Add the beans and cook for 2 more minutes, then add the zucchini and cook for an additional 2 to 3 minutes, until both the beans and the zucchini are crisp yet tender. Strain all the cooked vegetables into a colander and let sit to drain well, at least 3 minutes.

Add the hot vegetables to the mixing bowl, and add the olive oil, basil, salt, and cracked black pepper to taste. With a rubber spatula, toss gently to combine. The potatoes should break up into pieces and coat the vegetables.

SERVES 4 TO 6

▸ The curcubit family encompasses nearly a thousand species of cucumbers, melons, and squashes.

COSTATA ROMANESCO SQUASH

SQUASH BLOSSOM/CALABAZA

ZEPHYR SQUASH

PATTYPAN SQUASH

GOLDBAR SQUASH

YELLOW STRAIGHTNECK SQUASH

AVOCADO SQUASH

SAFARI SQUASH

BOOTHBY'S BLONDE CUCUMBER

KIRBY CUCUMBER

MEXICAN GHERKIN/MOUSE MELON

KOREAN CUCUMBER

WHITE KIRBY CUCUMBER

LEMON CUCUMBER

CHAMEH MELON

SNOW LEOPARD MELON

CHRISTMAS MELON

HONEY YELLOW MELON

CANTALOUPE

SUGAR BABY WATERMELON

Farmer STANLEY OSCZEPINSKI
S&SO PRODUCE

Sometimes when you're home from market washing a head of lettuce or a bunch of celery you find specks of soil as dark as squid ink. That's a sure sign that your food was grown in what's called the Black Dirt region, a patch of Orange County that looks like devil's food cake spread out for miles. It's some of the most fertile farmland in the country.

That fertility built up over millennia under a glacial lake that was still muckland a century ago. But Stanley Osczepinski's grandfather, who emigrated from Poland in 1921, was one of the farmers who dug ditches by hand and drained the swamps into the superb soils the region is now known for. In some places you have to dig down eighty feet before you'll hit a single stone.

Stanley grew up farming his grandfather's 17 acres with his dad, and like everyone in the area they specialized in one thing: onions. They sold their crop wholesale every October and had to make that money stretch a full year until the following fall's harvest. To help cover bills, they drove trucks on the side.

That all changed one day in 1976 when they got a phone call from a woman named Lys McLaughlin, inviting them to try something unusual: a farmers market opening in Manhattan. Their onions weren't ready, so they raided their family garden and showed up on day one with beets, carrots, lettuce, tomatoes, and peppers—all of which sold out by 11 a.m.

That first market was in a gated police parking lot near Bloomingdale's. The farmers arrived at 6 a.m. to set up, but manager Bob Lewis didn't open the gate to the public until 8.

◀ Stanley's grandfather dug ditches by hand, helping transform ancient muckland into black dirt: some of the most superb soil in the country.

"The people were so anxious to get in," Stanley recalled. "They were like a bunch of little kids at the fence holding on with their fingers. And once Bob opened the gates, they would charge. Like they had to get to the food that *second*."

"Going home through the Lincoln Tunnel," he remembers, "we said, 'Wow, we gotta try this again next week!' We went back, and it just kept growing and growing and growing." And because of that, their farm did, too.

While much is made of how Greenmarket changed the way New Yorkers eat, it also changed the way participating farmers farm. The Osczepinskis quickly set to planting new crops, and more the following year and the year after that, on more and more land, learning through trial and error, until their fields and market tables offered dill, cilantro, garlic, parsley root, black radishes, delicata squash, a dozen kinds of lettuce, radicchio, frisée, even artichokes, all of better quality—and better prices—than you can find in any supermarket.

Stanley's twin daughters, Allison and Keri, started coming to market with him when they were seven years old, and now Allison's husband, Mark, is Stanley's right-hand man on the farm. Today they farm a full 500 acres. But despite all the evolution, you'd better believe they still grow onions. Red onions, white onions, chives, garlic chives, scallions, red scallions, cipollini, Italian sweet flat red onions, and 12 acres of shallots. Perhaps the most beautiful are their leeks, which you can take home, slice open, and glimpse the powdery black gold that made it all possible.

PURSLANE-PEACH SALAD WITH FETA AND PICKLED RED ONIONS

by **MIKE PRICE, MARKET TABLE**

Over the years, some farmers have come to appreciate a harvest hidden in plain sight: weeds. While you don't want them crowding out your crops, wild plants can be delicious as they are pervasive, and for citizens of the urban jungle, there's something wonderful about feasting on foraged foods. Purslane, a summer succulent with crunchy, pink stems and fat, juicy leaves has gotten so popular that, ironically, some farmers now actually order seeds and plant the widely prized "weed."

If you can't find purslane, this salad is also wonderful with another wild edible: watercress. Either way, you'll love the pretty quick-pickled onions and creamy-tart feta. Best of all, the savory use of peaches lets you feast on the fruit before you even get to dessert.

Preheat the oven to 325°F.

In a small bowl, combine the shaved red onion, a pinch of sea salt, and the vinegar. Leave to marinate for at least one hour.

Meanwhile, make the croutons by tossing the cubed bread with 1 tablespoon of olive oil and salt and pepper to taste. Bake at 325°F for 10 to 12 minutes.

Once pickled, the onions will turn pink. Transfer them to a medium serving bowl, reserving the vinegar in the small bowl. While whisking, slowly drizzle the remaining 3 tablespoons olive oil into the vinegar to make a vinaigrette.

To the serving bowl, add the purslane, peaches, herbs, and feta. Dress with the vinaigrette, season with salt and pepper to taste, and toss lightly. Top with croutons and serve.

SERVES 4

1 SMALL RED ONION, SHAVED INTO ROUNDS

SEA SALT

¼ CUP SEASONED RICE WINE VINEGAR

¼ CUP DICED BREAD, ANY KIND, FROM PULLMAN TO PUMPERNICKEL, IN ¼-INCH CUBES

4 TABLESPOONS GOOD EXTRA VIRGIN OLIVE OIL, DIVIDED

FRESHLY GROUND BLACK PEPPER

8 OUNCES PURSLANE, ROUGHLY CHOPPED INTO BITE-SIZE PIECES

2 LARGE RIPE PEACHES

2 TABLESPOONS ROUGH CHOPPED HERBS, SUCH AS DILL, TARRAGON, CHIVES, CHERVIL, AND PARSLEY

4 OUNCES CRUMBLED FETA

BROWN BUTTER TOMATOES

by **AMANDA HESSER, FOOD52.COM AND PROVISIONS**

2 LARGE OR 3 SMALL RIPE BEEFSTEAK TOMATOES

6 TABLESPOONS UNSALTED BUTTER

FLAKY SEA SALT, SUCH AS MALDON

COARSELY GROUND BLACK PEPPER

BAGUETTE OR OTHER COUNTRY BREAD, FOR MOPPING UP THE BUTTER

Most locavores have more recipes for tomatoes than Eskimos have names for snow. But this preparation, which drizzles *beurre noisette* over tomatoes in place of the classic olive oil, will stop you in your tracks. As surprising as it is simple, it's the kind of thing you can slap together in mere minutes for a solo snack or serve to guests on fine china.

Core the tomatoes and slice them ⅓-inch thick. Divide the slices among four plates (preferably warmed), overlapping the slices just a little.

Place the butter in a small, heavy-bottomed saucepan and set over medium heat. Let the butter melt completely. It will begin bubbling. Let the butter simmer away, cooking off its water, until it begins to smell nutty and brown, 3 to 5 minutes. Swirl the pan every 30 seconds or so. When the butter turns the color of a hazelnut, remove it from the heat. Use a soup spoon to ladle it over the tomatoes. They'll sizzle! You want to dress the tomatoes with the butter, as if you were pouring ganache over a cake—be generous!

Season the tomatoes with salt and pepper, then rush the plates to the table so everyone can taste the tomatoes while the butter is hot. Mop up the butter and tomato juices with good bread. Toast to summer!

SERVES 4

GRILLED OKRA WITH FENNEL SEEDS AND FRESH OREGANO

by **SISHA ORTUZAR, RIVERPARK**

Chef Ortuzar is a committed market shopper, but he's the rare Manhattanite with access to vegetables even fresher than what he can buy at farm stands. That's because his restaurant grows much of its own produce, steps from the kitchen.

A skyscraper is an unlikely spot for agriculture, but the staff partnered with GrowNYC to set up hundreds of milk crates, holding upstate soil and home to crops that would make a homesteader green with envy. A full-time farmer tends everything from eggplant to watermelon, but Ortuzar has a soft spot for okra. He grills it with merken—a smoked, ground chili pepper from his native Santiago, which we approximate here with spice cabinet standards. The quick cooking yields no slipperiness, winning over even okra skeptics.

1 GARLIC CLOVE

2 TABLESPOONS OLIVE OIL, DIVIDED, PLUS MORE FOR TOASTING GARLIC

1 POUND FRESH OKRA

2 TEASPOONS SEA SALT

1 TABLESPOON FENNEL SEEDS

2 TEASPOONS MERKEN OR SMOKED PIMENTON PLUS 1 TEASPOON GROUND CORIANDER

¼ CUP FRESH PARSLEY

1 TABLESPOON FRESH OREGANO

ZEST OF 1 LEMON

Toast the garlic: Slice the garlic lengthwise as thinly as possible, ideally using a mandolin to shave it ¹⁄₁₆-inch thick. Place it in your smallest saucepan and cover with enough oil to lift the garlic off the bottom of the pan. Cook at a very low simmer, taking care not to let the oil boil or the garlic burn. The garlic will brown slowly and, when toasted, will rise to the surface of the oil. Remove the garlic from the oil and drain it on a paper towel. Reserve the oil to cook the okra or for another use.

Cook the okra: Preheat a grill or cast-iron skillet over medium-high heat until very hot. In a large mixing bowl, toss the okra with 2 teaspoons of olive oil and the sea salt.

Place the okra on the grill or in the skillet and sear for 3 to 4 minutes on each side, until they develop a nice char all over. Return the okra to the bowl and toss gently with the toasted garlic, fennel seeds, *merken*, parsley and oregano, lemon zest, 1 tablespoon of olive oil, and more sea salt to taste.

SERVES 4 AS A SIDE DISH

◀ Chef Ortuzar's restaurant Riverpark boasts an urban farm overlooking FDR Drive. (Amanda Gentile)

SQUASH SALAD WITH RADISHES, MANCHEGO, AND LEMON VINAIGRETTE

by **SEAMUS MULLEN, TERTULIA**

2½ POUNDS MIXED SUMMER SQUASH AND ZUCCHINI, VARIOUS SHAPES, SIZES, AND VARIETIES

1 PEELED SHALLOT

1 BUNCH MIXED RADISHES, GREEN STEMS REMOVED, SCRUBBED CLEAN

1 FINELY MINCED GARLIC CLOVE

1 TABLESPOON HONEY

JUICE AND ZEST OF 2 LEMONS, ABOUT 2 TEASPOONS ZEST AND 4 TABLESPOONS JUICE

2 TABLESPOONS CHAMPAGNE VINEGAR OR SWEET WHITE WINE VINEGAR

1 TABLESPOON KOSHER SALT

FRESH CRACKED PEPPER

½ CUP EXTRA VIRGIN OLIVE OIL

1 TABLESPOON GRATED FRESH HORSERADISH

½ CUP BASIL LEAVES, TORN INTO SMALL PIECES

½ CUP MINT LEAVES, TORN INTO SMALL PIECES

2 OUNCES FINELY GRATED MANCHEGO CHEESE, ABOUT 1 CUP

Go ahead and fold back this page now, because you're going to want to make this bright, gorgeously fresh recipe all summer long. Simply shave raw summer squash and radishes on a mandolin, whisk together a quick, citrusy vinaigrette, shower with grated Manchego, and finish with handfuls of basil and mint.

You can use squash standbys such as zucchini and crookneck in this recipe, but it's even more beautiful with a mix of colors and shapes, from sunny yellow pattypans to ridged Romanescos to the perfectly round, aptly named eight-ball. Some farmers grow horseradish root, which grows straight and deep and has wonderful heat when grated fresh, but if you can't find it for this dressing, prepared horseradish works just fine.

Set a mandolin on the thinnest setting. Slice the squash, shallot, and radishes crosswise into thin coins. Transfer to a large mixing bowl and toss gently to combine.

In a small mixing bowl, whisk together the garlic, honey, lemon juice, vinegar, salt, and pepper. While whisking, steadily drizzle in the olive oil to form a vinaigrette.

Add the lemon vinaigrette to the squash mixture and toss gently. Finish the salad with lemon zest, horseradish, basil and mint, a generous sprinkle of grated cheese, and additional salt and pepper to taste. Gently toss to combine and serve.

SERVES 4

ROMANO

LIMA

FAVA

CRANBERRY

HARICOT VERTS

LONG BEANS

FRESH POLE BEAN SALAD

by DANNY AMEND AND JOHN ADLER, FRANNY'S AND MARCO'S

Franny's in Brooklyn is famous for its wood-oven pizza, but the vegetable sides alone are worth the trip to Flatbush Avenue. As longtime shoppers of the Grand Army Plaza Greenmarket, the restaurant's produce preparations are simple but spectacular, relying not on overwrought preparations but on sparklingly fresh ingredients.

Take this salad of pole beans such as Romano, Kentucky Wonder, or Scarlet Wonders—all of which require trellising but whose flavors easily best the more common bush beans. After a quick blanching, they're dressed with an easy vinaigrette, mild summer onions, toasted pistachios, and a slightly salty grated goat cheese. Chef Adler calls the combination "the essence of summer"—little wonder it's one of the restaurant's most popular dishes.

¼ CUP RED WINE VINEGAR

⅓ CUP EXTRA VIRGIN OLIVE OIL

1 MEDIUM RED ONION, PEELED AND SLICED INTO ⅛-INCH THICK SLICES

1 TEASPOON SALT

8 TO 10 CRACKS OF FRESHLY GROUND BLACK PEPPER

4 OUNCES COARSELY GRATED PANTALEO CHEESE (A SARDINIAN GOAT MILK CHEESE, OR OTHER HARD GRATING CHEESE), DIVIDED

1½ POUNDS MIXED POLE BEANS, SUCH AS GREEN, WAX, AND ROMANO BEANS, STEMS REMOVED

¾ CUP SHELLED, TOASTED, AND CHOPPED PISTACHIOS, DIVIDED

Bring a large pot of water to a boil. Season generously with salt until it tastes like the ocean. Prepare a large bowl with ice water.

While waiting for the water to boil, combine the red wine vinegar, olive oil, onion, salt, pepper, and half of the grated cheese in a large serving bowl. Mix well and let marinate as you prepare the beans.

When the water boils, add the pole beans and blanch 2 to 3 minutes until softened, but still maintaining a bit of a crunch. Drain and immediately add to the ice water to shock. Once cooled, remove and dry on a tea towel.

Add the beans and half of the pistachios to the dressing. Toss well to combine. Top with additional cheese and pistachios before serving.

SERVES 6

CHILLED TOMATO SOUP WITH CORN SALAD

by **RALF KUETTEL, TRESTLE ON TENTH**

Soup

4 LARGE, RIPE TOMATOES,
ANY VARIETY

2 RIPE PLUM TOMATOES

1 ROUGHLY CHOPPED GARLIC
CLOVE

3 TABLESPOONS EXTRA VIRGIN
OLIVE OIL

2 TABLESPOONS RED WINE
VINEGAR, DIVIDED

3 DASHES TOBASCO,
OR SIMILAR HOT SAUCE

SALT AND FRESHLY GROUND
BLACK PEPPER

Salad

¾ CUP CORN KERNELS, SHUCKED
FROM 1 EAR OF FRESH CORN

1 SMALL CUCUMBER, SEEDED
AND DICED

6 LARGE BASIL LEAVES, CUT INTO
RIBBONS

1 TABLESPOON EXTRA VIRGIN
OLIVE OIL

1 TABLESPOON LEMON JUICE,
FROM ½ LEMON

SALT AND FRESHLY GROUND
BLACK PEPPER

A celebration of summer, this soup makes refreshing use of tomatoes, corn, cucumbers, and basil. Think of it as an American answer to gazpacho.

Use any varieties of tomatoes, from hybrids such as Early Girl to heirlooms like Brandywine or Black Krim, as long as they're perfectly ripe. Pureed raw, the ingredients retain their bright flavors—without heating up your kitchen.

Don't skip the garnish. Many market shoppers are surprised to learn that corn can be eaten raw, and it's true, the less-fresh stuff on supermarket shelves wouldn't be enjoyable uncooked. But when the ears are just one day off the stalk—or, in the case of Sycamore Farms, picked that very morning—the kernels are so fresh, you can just peel back the husks and enjoy the sweet juiciness. Or cut them off the cob for this sparkling corn salad.

Prepare the soup: Halve and seed the tomatoes, then cut them into 1-inch dice. In a medium mixing bowl, combine the diced tomatoes with the garlic, olive oil, 1 tablespoon of the vinegar, and hot sauce. Season with salt and pepper to taste, as if you were eating the tomatoes raw. Mix well, cover, and refrigerate for 18 to 24 hours to marinate.

Pour the entire contents of the bowl into a blender and puree on high until smooth, about 2 minutes. Season to taste with salt, pepper, and the remaining tablespoon of vinegar. Refrigerate until ready to serve.

Make the salad: In a medium bowl, combine the corn, cucumber, basil, olive oil, and lemon juice. Season to taste with salt and pepper.

To serve: Pour the chilled soup into a shallow bowl. Add a mound of corn salad in the center of the soup. Garnish with an additional sprinkle of salt and a drizzle of olive oil.

SERVES 4

BROCCOLI WITH PISTACHIOS, CHILES, AND MINT

by **RON GALLO, JOJO**

This recipe only takes a few minutes to make, combining summer standbys into a surprising dish you'll return to again and again. Chef Gallo dresses up blanched broccoli with a quick crown of sizzled garlic, pistachios, chile, and mint, yielding great garlic flavor, the crunch of nuts, and the heat of the jalapeño, while the quick-fried mint becomes wonderfully crisp. Serve it straight or alongside fish or meat—but be prepared for this simple side to steal the show.

Bring an 8-quart stockpot of water to boil and season well with salt. Cut the broccoli into spears, leaving the stems on, about ½-inch thick. Blanch the broccoli in the boiling water and cook until the stems are crisp-tender, 3 to 4 minutes. Drain well in a colander and arrange on a serving platter.

Heat a 10-inch skillet over medium heat. Add the olive oil then garlic and sauté until pale golden, about 1 minute. Add the pistachios and cook 1 more minute. Add the jalapeño and mint and sauté until the mint is crispy and aromatic. Remove from the heat, season with a pinch of salt, and immediately spoon the mixture over the broccoli. Finish with fresh lemon zest and juice.

SERVES 4

1 HEAD BROCCOLI WITH 2-INCH STEM, ABOUT 1 POUND

¼ CUP EXTRA VIRGIN OLIVE OIL

3 THINLY SLICED GARLIC CLOVES

¼ CUP ROUGHLY CHOPPED, RAW PISTACHIOS

1 SMALL, THINLY SLICED JALAPEÑO

½ CUP ROUGHLY CHOPPED, GENTLY PACKED MINT LEAVES

SALT

ZEST AND JUICE OF 1 LEMON, ABOUT 2 TABLESPOONS JUICE

Farmer SERGIO NOLASCO
NOLASCO'S FARM

Once a week an unlikely oasis appears on a stretch of concrete just outside a scrubby park in the Bronx: tables overflowing with produce as fresh as you can find anywhere in America. While the Bronx suffers from some of the highest rates of obesity and diet-related disease in the country, every Tuesday, July through November, shoppers line up at the corner of 192nd Street and Grand Concourse a good hour before the market's official 8 a.m. opening time. Many are waiting for one farmer in particular—Sergio Nolasco.

Like many of these customers, Sergio grew up on a farm in Mexico. But today he farms in New Jersey, growing standards such as tomatoes, lettuce, potatoes, and onions, plus ingredients only recently eaten by Americans—cilantro and tomatillos—as well as herbs that are virtually unavailable in America: *papalo*, a succulent green that's often tucked into tortillas; *pepiche*, whose velvety leaves perfume cemita sandwiches; *alache*, whose long green leaves are popular in Puebla; *quelites*, a cousin of amaranth; and *epazote*, which seasons pots of beans simmering over open fires and uptown hot plates. By September, he'll harvest a dozen different chiles, from dark green poblanos for stuffing to orange habañeros that should come with a warning label in English.

Sergio immigrated to New York at age fourteen in search of economic opportunity but was soon working a dead-end sweatshop job in a garment factory. He was desperate for the chance to build a better life.

He found it in the form of Greenmarket's New Farmer Development Project (NFDP), which helps

◀ *Latino shoppers line up for Sergio's pepiche and papalo, which are all but unavailable in America.* (Amanda Gentile)

immigrants with previous agricultural experience put down farming roots here.

When a friend of Sergio's read about the project in an article in *El Diario* in 2004, Sergio jumped at the chance to empower himself through agriculture and become a small business owner. In 2005 he enrolled in the program's class for new farmers—and had a lot to learn. Sure, he'd grown up on his grandfather's farm, but childhood memories of plowing sugarcane fields with oxen have limited stateside application.

So-called experts say low-income neighborhoods have little demand for fresh produce, but Sergio knows otherwise.

So before he was ready to farm on his own, Sergio spent four years learning the ropes under an NFDP partner farm in the Hudson Valley, where he mastered diverse vegetable crops in the few months before spring's last frost and fall's first. Through NFDP, he received an eight thousand dollar micro-credit loan that he used to purchase a small tractor, some row cover, and seeds.

Finally he and his family were ready to farm on their own. Now they rent 40 gorgeous acres in New Jersey, farming more than fifty diverse varieties from Romaine lettuce to Caribbean callaloo.

Today other immigrants are sharing in the fruits of these labors. Sergio sells at Poe Park in the Bronx and other Greenmarkets in underserved Latino communities: Manhattan's Washington Heights and nearby Inwood, plus Sunnyside and Jackson Heights, in Queens. For him, selling in these communities isn't good karma, it's good business. So-called experts say low-income neighborhoods have little demand for fresh produce, but Sergio knows otherwise. His customers cook every night, often for big families. And when they find good produce at a fair price—especially the traditional foods they grew up eating—they line up to buy by the pound.

So while everyone else at Poe Park on this blistering morning is looking for a spot of shade, Sergio doesn't mind the heat. By 2 p.m., the only thing left on his table will be the last drooping handful of cilantro, and he'll have an apron full of cash. Exhausted, he'll pack up the tent and price signs and drive back to New Jersey to get in a few more hours of farming before dusk. For dinner, he'll feed his children the foods his grandparents fed his parents almost three thousand miles away, and tomorrow he'll be up with the sun to harvest.

It may not be everyone's idea of the American Dream, but it is Sergio's. And he's living it.

TOMATILLO-MINT SALSA

by **SUE TORRES, SUEÑOS**

1½ POUNDS TOMATILLOS, HUSKS DISCARDED, WASHED, ROUGHLY CHOPPED, ABOUT 3½ CUPS

½ CUP PEELED, ROUGHLY CHOPPED YELLOW ONION

4 PEELED, ROUGHLY CHOPPED GARLIC CLOVES

1 SERRANO CHILE, STEM REMOVED, HALVED LENGTHWISE

½ CUP MINT LEAVES

SALT TO TASTE

If you think salsa's defining ingredients are tomatoes and cilantro, this tomatillo-mint version will change your mind forever.

Due to the chile company they keep, many people mistakenly think tomatillos are fiery, but in truth their flavor is citrusy bright, not spicy. And while they can be eaten raw, here they're simmered with a serrano pepper until they collapse completely, then pureed with mint.

A word about how heat (temperature) affects heat (spiciness): Served warm, the chile brings an extra burn. Chilled, it's milder. So if you want to turn down the burn, make this one day ahead and serve it cold. Either way, with each bite you'll bounce between the chile's heat and the cooling mint, and back again.

In a small pot combine everything but the mint with 1¼ cups of water. Bring to a low simmer and cook, covered, over low heat for 25 minutes. Allow to cool, then puree in a blender with the mint. Add salt to taste.

PICKLED "MEAN BEANS"

by RICK FIELD, RICK'S PICKS

9 PEELED GARLIC CLOVES (3 CLOVES PER JAR)

1½ TEASPOONS CAYENNE PEPPER (½ TEASPOON PER JAR)

3 TABLESPOONS DILL SEED (1 TABLESPOON PER JAR)

9 SPRIGS FRESH DILL (3 SPRIGS PER JAR)

1½ POUNDS GREEN BEANS

1⅔ CUPS WHITE VINEGAR

1 TABLESPOON PLUS 2 TEASPOONS KOSHER SALT

Rick Field was working as a producer at PBS when Saturdays at Brooklyn's Grand Army Plaza Greenmarket inspired him to get back into something from his childhood summers in Vermont: pickling. Soon his apartment was stacked to the ceiling with more glass jars than a farmhouse pantry, but his flavor concoctions were decidedly urban. After some serious research (read: "pickle parties") he decided to go pro, selling from a table next to the farmers whose produce he buys by the case. Jars of aromatic "Phat Beets" and pimentón-perfumed "Smokra" draw crowds, but one of the most enduringly popular offerings is this one, a riff on dilly beans that uses twice the cayenne of his parents' version. As Rick explains, "The kids like things hot."

If fresh flowering dill is available, you're in luck. Substitute one head per jar for the dill seed and sprigs.

Divide the garlic cloves, cayenne, dill seed, and dill into 3 pint-size mason jars. Wash the beans, line them in stacks, and trim each stack to about 4 inches. Pack the beans vertically and snugly into the jars, tails down.

In a small saucepan, make the brine: combine 1⅔ cups of water with the vinegar and salt, bring just to a boil, then let cool to 190°F. Pour the brine over the beans.

To can, place lids on the jars and process in a boiling water bath for 7 minutes. Or, for refrigerator pickles, simply stick in the fridge. Either way, allow 2 to 4 weeks for flavors to combine before eating.

MAKES 3 PINTS

SUMMER SUCCOTASH

by **JOHN CONLIN, TANGLED VINE**

Although this riff on succotash—the traditional corn-lima combination first eaten by East Coast Native Americans—is spiked with chile peppers, it's not at all hot. That's because Grenada peppers—one of the hundreds of capsicums Tim Stark grows at Eckerton Hill Farm and picks each August and September—have fantastic flavor but next to no heat. (They're in the group chefs call "seasoning peppers." But don't worry, if you want off-the-charts hot, Tim grows those, too.)

If you can't find a Grenada pepper, you could substitute a diced, seeded jalapeño, but a better fit would be half of a Scotch bonnet or habañero, seeded and blanched to put out the fire. Either way, this side is excellent with summer fish, especially striped bass.

1 CUP FRESH, SHELLED LIMA BEANS

1 TABLESPOON VEGETABLE OIL

1½ CUPS OKRA, ABOUT ⅓ POUND, STEMS TRIMMED, HALVED LENGTHWISE

4 TABLESPOONS UNSALTED BUTTER, DIVIDED

1 MEDIUM, FINELY DICED YELLOW ONION

4 CUPS CORN KERNELS, CUT FROM ABOUT 3 TO 4 EARS OF FRESH CORN

1 CUP GRAPE TOMATOES, HALVED

2 THINLY SLICED GRENADA PEPPERS (SEE HEADNOTE)

1 TEASPOON FINELY CHOPPED FRESH MARJORAM

SALT

JUICE OF 1 LIME

Bring a small saucepan of water to a boil. Season well with salt and blanch the lima beans until crisp tender, about 2 minutes. Drain and rinse well.

Heat a large, heavy-bottomed skillet over medium-high heat and add the vegetable oil. When the oil begins to smoke lightly, add the okra, cut side down and season with a pinch of salt. Cook about 2 minutes and flip. Continue to cook for 1 more minute or until the okra is just cooked through and tender. The okra should be well colored and lightly charred. Remove from the pan and place on a paper towel to drain any excess oil.

Return the skillet to medium heat. Add 2 tablespoons of butter and heat until foamy. Add the onion and sauté until translucent, about 4 minutes. Increase heat to high and add the corn. (If using jalapeño in place of Grenada pepper, add now). Season with salt and sauté until the corn is just cooked through, about 5 minutes, stirring occasionally.

Add the tomatoes, blanched limas, and fried okra, then the remaining 2 tablespoons of butter, tossing constantly to coat. Add the Grenada pepper, if using, and the marjoram, tossing to incorporate. Adjust seasoning, squeeze a lime over the top, and serve.

SERVES 4

STRIPED BASS WITH SUMMER BEANS AND HEIRLOOM TOMATOES

by **PRESTON MADSON, FREEMANS**

2 TABLESPOONS EXTRA VIRGIN OLIVE OIL, DIVIDED

4 5-OUNCE FILLETS STRIPED BASS

½ POUND GREEN BEANS, TRIMMED AND HALVED

2 SLICED GARLIC CLOVES

1 MEDIUM PEELED AND SLICED SHALLOT

1 TABLESPOON THYME LEAVES

2 LARGE HEIRLOOM TOMATOES, DICED, JUICES RESERVED

SALT AND PEPPER TO TASTE

HALF A LEMON

This simple two-skillet meal is the quintessential East Coast summer dish.

Silvery sleek "stripers" live much of their lives in the Atlantic but chase spawning shad up the Hudson River each spring. Long prized by the Lenape, these fish have been one of the most important fisheries from North Carolina to Maine for centuries. In recent years, their population has rebounded, thanks to commercial restrictions. You can eat striped bass in good conscience—Atlantic striped bass caught by hook and line is a "Best Choice" of the Seafood Watch Program.

Highly versatile, striped bass takes well to steaming, grilling, baking whole, and even deep-frying. In this recipe, Chef Preston panfries fillets for a simple and quick preparation that showcases the fish's firm flesh and superb flavor.

Preheat the oven to 400°F.

Heat a 12-inch oven-safe sauté pan over medium-high heat. Add 1 table-spoon of olive oil to coat the bottom. Season the fish with salt and pepper and place in the pan skin side down. Cook for 4 to 5 minutes or until the skin is crispy. Transfer to the oven until just cooked through, 8 to 10 minutes.

Meanwhile, heat another 12-inch skillet over medium-high heat. Add the remaining tablespoon of olive oil and the green beans, season with salt and pepper, and cook until slightly charred, 3 to 4 minutes. Add the garlic, shal-lot, and thyme. Add the tomato and its juices and cook until the tomato stews down, 2 to 3 minutes. Season with salt and pepper to taste.

Serve the stewed tomatoes and green beans in a shallow bowl and top with the striped bass. Finish with a squeeze of lemon.

SERVES 4

SUMMER PASTA WITH SUNGOLD TOMATOES

by **ED LEVINE, SERIOUSEATS.COM**

As a kid you learned that, botanically speaking, tomatoes are a fruit. And you'll finally think of them that way once you sink your teeth into a Sungold.

A hybrid variety of cherry tomato, they're sold by the pint and easy to miss, but pop one in your mouth and you'll soon be asking for these orange-hued hybrids by name. They definitely don't require a recipe—it's hard not to eat them all on the way home from the market—but longtime tastemaker Ed Levine captures their sweet-tart, tomato-candy flavor in this simple-but-spectacular summer pasta. Ed buys his tomatoes at the Tucker Square Greenmarket near his Upper West Side home, but Sungolds have found fame at markets across the country and are worth seeking out for this preparation, which requires zero technique, only great ingredients. As Ed explains, "As long as the tomatoes are good, nobody can screw it up."

8 OUNCES FUSILLI OR OTHER SHORT, STURDY PASTA

3 TABLESPOONS EXTRA VIRGIN OLIVE OIL

2 PINTS PERFECTLY RIPE SUNGOLD CHERRY TOMATOES, HALVED

¼ CUP ROUGHLY CHOPPED BASIL LEAVES

FRESHLY GROUND BLACK PEPPER

KOSHER SALT

FRESH MOZZARELLA OR GRATED PARMIGIANO-REGGIANO (OPTIONAL)

Bring a large pot of salted water to a boil and cook the pasta according to package directions, just until al dente. Drain the pasta in a colander, then run under cold water until chilled. Drain well and transfer to a large bowl.

Add the olive oil, tomatoes, and basil, and toss to combine. Season to taste with salt and black pepper. Garnish with cubes of mozzarella or grated Parmigiano-Reggiano, if desired.

SERVES 4

LAMB BURGERS WITH TZATZIKI AND ARUGULA

by **KAREN WEINBERG, 3-CORNER FIELD FARM**

Tzatziki

1½ CUPS SHEEP'S MILK YOGURT
(CAN SUBSTITUTE WHOLE MILK
YOGURT)

1 SMALL KIRBY CUCUMBER,
HALVED AND SEEDED

2 FINELY CHOPPED GARLIC SCAPES

1 TABLESPOON CHOPPED MINT

1 LIME

Burgers

2 POUNDS GROUND LAMB
OR MUTTON

6 ENGLISH MUFFINS OR BRIOCHE
BUNS

2 CUPS BABY ARUGULA

SALT AND FRESHLY GROUND
BLACK PEPPER

Where's the beef? Who cares? This lamb burger, dressed in a mint-garlic-yogurt sauce, is fresher and far more flavorful.

Karen Weinberg raises 100 percent grass-fed lamb, making the mama ewes' milk into yogurt and feta, both of which pair beautifully with this burger. And while the young male "ram lambs" born to her flock are sold as mild meat, the more mature mutton has terrific flavor Karen prefers in her own burger.

When it comes to forming patties, don't over flatten them. You want the outside seared but the middle rare and juicy, so leave the center a good inch thick. Karen paints a little tamari on the surface to make a slightly salty crust, but skip this if you'll put her sheep's feta on the burger, which will bring its own saltiness.

Of course these burgers are great on the grill, but Karen always tells customers to buy a cheap cast-iron skillet or griddle. And there's no need to add oil to the pan. Her lamb typically runs about 90 percent lean—enough fat, on medium heat, so the meat doesn't stick.

Place the yogurt in a cheesecloth-lined strainer or colander, set over a bowl, and strain for 4 hours in the refrigerator to thicken the yogurt.

Finely dice the cucumber, transfer to a colander, and season with ½ teaspoon of salt. Let drain for one hour. Transfer to a bowl and add the yogurt, garlic scapes, mint, lime zest and juice. Season with salt and pepper.

Prepare the burgers: Divide the lamb into six 1-inch patties. Heat a grill pan or cast-iron skillet over medium-high heat, and add 2 to 3 patties to the dry pan. Do not crowd the pan. Cook for 3 to 4 minutes per side for medium-rare. Remove from heat and let rest for five minutes. Repeat with remaining patties. Serve on toasted buns with tzatziki and a handful of baby arugula.

SERVES 6

Fishers ALEX AND STEPHANIE VILLANI

BLUE MOON FISH

New York City has a long history of fishmongers, from the 191-year-old Fulton Fish Market to female pushcart peddlers of the early twentieth century who hawked cod, yellow pike, and whitefish through the Lower East Side's dense alleys.

Yet these sellers have always been several steps removed from the fishers themselves. Since 1988 Alex Villani and Blue Moon Fish have challenged that model, bringing the fish—and the fisherman—directly from the seas to Greenmarket customers, offering what is widely hailed as the freshest seafood in the city.

After spending his childhood in a five-story walkup in Chelsea, Villani and his family moved to Copiague, Long Island. He returned to the city for some desultory study at City College, but was soon back on Long Island where he found work as a clammer. After years on commercial boats, often spending days at a time at sea. In 1992 he bought a Maine-built, 35-foot boat kitted out to fish alone. Its name: the Blue Moon.

Villani's sister, Diane, who lives in downtown Manhattan, knew of her brother's experience selling his catch to wholesalers: They were certainly convenient, but the paycheck often didn't go far—Villani jokes he only made a profit "once in a blue moon"—so Diane recommended he experiment with selling his own fish, directly to the customer, at the Greenmarket.

The side venture soon became Villani's big kahuna. While most fish counters today offer seas of species that are endangered, have been flown frozen from

◀ *Blue Moon's fish is widely hailed as the freshest in the city. Alex lands it all himself in the clean, cold waters off Long Island.* (Amanda Gentile)

(Amanda Gentile)

distant ports, or both, Blue Moon's customers queue up in long lines, awaiting their turn to buy spectacularly fresh porgy, fluke, squid, hake, striped bass, monkfish, herring, mussels, and sometimes lobster—all of which Villani landed himself in the clean, cold waters off Long Island.

While seafood choices are often imported, frozen, or both, Blue Moon brings the catch— and the captain—directly from the shore to the city.

But selling his just-caught fish directly to eaters didn't only transform his livelihood, it also changed his life, in the form of a fellow vendor who would become his partner in seafood and love.

Stephanie Villani had recently graduated from NYU and was toiling at a small literary magazine with a commensurately small budget when a friend suggested she earn extra cash with a Saturday shift for an apple farmer whose stand happened to be right next to Blue Moon's. Vendors would sometimes go out for a drink after a long day's selling, but one afternoon, it was just the two of them. Soon Stephanie moved to Mattituck on Long Island's North Fork, where Alex docked the Blue Moon and where they now have a solar-powered home and a joyful little girl named Ruby.

Stephanie and Alex drive into the city together early each Saturday morning, but on Wednesdays, Stephanie comes to Union Square solo, allowing Alex to get out on the water with his orange oilers. For him, one day away from the waters is enough. The rest of the week, he heeds the call of the sea.

ROASTED BLUEFISH WITH PICKLED PEACHES, SWEET CORN, AND OPAL BASIL

by **RYAN ANGULO, BUTTERMILK CHANNEL**

3 PEACHES

1 EAR CORN

1 BUNCH SCALLIONS (ABOUT 8 SCALLIONS)

1 RED BELL PEPPER

2 KIRBY CUCUMBERS

¼ BUNCH OPAL BASIL, LEAVES ONLY

2 FRESH HOT CHILES (JALAPEÑOS, SERRANOS, OR SCOTCH BONNET)

2 CUPS CIDER VINEGAR

1½ CUPS SUGAR

1 TABLESPOON SEA SALT

2 POUNDS BONELESS BLUEFISH FILLETS, SKIN ON, CUT INTO 4 EQUAL PORTIONS

OLIVE OIL

SALT AND FRESHLY GROUND BLACK PEPPER

Bluefish are abundant in local waters all summer long and well into fall, but the species has something of a fishy reputation. It's true that if the fatty fish has been on land too long, its high oil content takes on a strong flavor. But if you catch yours at market just a day out of the water, the flesh will be fresh and flavorful. Gray-blue when raw, it turns off-white when cooked, and its high omega-3 fatty acids make it both healthful and hearty.

Here a cornucopia of high-summer produce, from peaches to peppers, takes a bath in a quick pickling liquid. What the produce loses in color it gains in assertive acidity, which stands up to the rich bluefish. Roasted with just a drizzle of oil, it's finished in ten minutes or less. (You could even skip the pickle—roasted bluefish is irresistable alongside anything from fresh tomatoes to fried potatoes.)

Blues are also great on the grill, if you've got one. Start them skin-side down, cook until the skin is crispy, then flip to finish.

Prep the produce: Pit the peaches and finely slice. Cut the corn kernels from the cob. Cut the scallions into 3-inch long batons. Halve the bell pepper lengthwise, discard the seeds and ribs, and slice into batons, about ⅛-inch thick. Slice the cucumbers into thin rounds. Cut the basil into thin strips. If using jalapeños or serranos, slice into very thin rings leaving the seeds intact. If using Scotch bonnets, cut in half, discard seeds and any white ribs, then finely slice (a pair of rubber gloves is recommended when dealing with hot chiles). Combine all vegetables in a large bowl but reserve a few pinches of basil for garnish.

Make the "pickle": Combine the vinegar, sugar, salt, and 2 cups of water in a pot and heat until the sugar has dissolved. Pour the hot liquid over the vegetables. Press plastic wrap onto the surface of the vegetables to keep them submerged and let cool.

Prepare the bluefish: Preheat the oven to 400°F and brush a foil-lined baking sheet with olive oil. Set the bluefish skin-side up on the sheet, drizzle with a little olive oil, and season with salt and pepper. Roast for 8 to 10 minutes, until the flesh turns a whitish-gray. Turn oven up to broil, and cook another minute or so, until the skin just starts to char.

Serve each fillet over a portion of the "pickle," garnished with additional basil.

TEA-MARINATED QUAIL WITH YOGURT, PICKLED ONIONS, AND CHARRED CHERRIES

by **JUSTIN SMILLIE, IL BUCO ALIMENTARI & VINERIA**

Quail

¼ CUP ROASTED BARLEY GENMAICHA GREEN TEA

¼ CUP EXTRA VIRGIN OLIVE OIL

2 TABLESPOONS AGED BALSAMIC

ZEST OF 1 LEMON

FRESHLY GROUND BLACK PEPPER

4 WHOLE QUAIL

Pickled Torpedo Onions

3 TORPEDO ONIONS

¼ CUP BROWN SUGAR

⅛ CUP SALT

½ CUP CHAMPAGNE VINEGAR

½ CUP RICE WINE VINEGAR

1 BAY LEAF

3 TABLESPOONS TOASTED CORIANDER SEEDS

PEEL OF 1 LEMON

1 THINLY SLICED GARLIC CLOVE

Once you realize how quickly quail cooks, you might decide not to heat up the kitchen for roast chicken, at least until fall. Each little butterflied bird serves one, but first they get a daylong flavor boost from nutty genmaicha tea, which can be found in most supermarkets. Here it's not brewed—simply snip open the tea bag and stir the dried contents together with olive oil and vinegar for a quick paste that's easy and aromatic.

This recipe calls for several components, but not one is complicated, and together the finished dish—complete with seasoned yogurt, pistachios, and pickled onions—is as beautiful as anything you can order on a white tablecloth. The garnishing charred cherries are wonderfully jammy and cook up in two minutes flat.

Make ahead: In a bowl, mix the genmaicha green tea with the olive oil, balsamic vinegar, lemon zest, and black pepper, until it forms a tight paste. Slather the marinade onto the quail and allow it to rest dry in the refrigerator for 24 hours.

To pickle the onions, slice them into rings and pack into a clean glass jar or other nonreactive container. In a small saucepan, heat the sugar and salt in ½ cup of water to dissolve. Remove from heat, then add the vinegars, bay leaf, coriander, lemon peel, and garlic. Pour the hot pickling liquid over the onions, cover, and let sit for at least 24 hours in the refrigerator to pickle.

To finish: Heat a cast-iron skillet over medium heat, and cook each marinated quail, one at a time, breast-side down until golden brown and crispy, about 3 to 4 minutes. Flip the bird and cook the other side for an additional 2 to 3 minutes. The flesh will be a lovely blush pink.

Let the skillet cool slightly, then wipe it clean and return to medium heat. Place the cherries cut side down in the dry skillet and caramelize for 1 to 2 minutes.

Season the yogurt with a few grinds of fresh black pepper. Place each quail on a plate, drizzle with seasoned yogurt, and top with cherries, pistachios, and pickled onions.

SERVES 4

Charred Cherries

12 SWEET CHERRIES, PITTED AND HALVED

½ CUP PLAIN GREEK YOGURT

FRESHLY GROUND BLACK PEPPER

3 TABLESPOONS CRUSHED PISTACHIOS

Farmer JOHN GORZYNSKI
GORZYNSKI ORNERY FARM

Many customers come to Greenmarket for organic ingredients, seeking out that certification on stand signs. But each Saturday at Union Square, the most impassioned ecological eaters can be found buying food from a farm that gave up its organic certification more than a decade ago.

Back in the 1970s, John Gorzynski was a tree surgeon in New Jersey and spent much of his time spraying pesticides to control everything from Dutch Elm disease to gypsy moths. But over the decade he saw his coworkers get cancer. He read Rachel Carson's famous book *Silent Spring*. And he observed, year after year, increased illness in the places that had received the most potent chemical applications.

"I came to see there was a natural system, natural controls," he recalls. "These sprays were disrupting that natural system. I realized it was bad on every possible level." So he quit and, to make a living, turned his hobby garden into a market garden, vowing to never use the kinds of chemicals that he had firsthand seen destroy human health and the wild environment.

In 1979 he started selling at the Gansevoort Greenmarket.

"By 1982 I realized I could make a living, so I bought my own farm and got married. And that's either the end or beginning of the story, depending on how you look at it."

But John wasn't just busy with his own farm. He dedicated decades to raising awareness about the

◄ *John believes in the kind of farming that lacks an easy adjective. When customers ask whether he's organic, most are more than happy with his complicated answer.* (Amanda Gentile)

perils of pesticides, educating the public about organic agriculture, and calling upon the federal government to regulate the use of the term to ensure strict standards customers could trust. He was a founding member of the New York chapter of the Northeast Organic Farming Association (NOFA) and was its chairman when it became a certification agency. And he was his county's Farm Bureau president from 1983 to 2001, voicing the concerns of organic farmers in that more conventional arena. "I was trying to be a level-headed person within the realm of chemically addicted people."

John wasn't just busy with his own farm. He dedicated decades to raising awareness about the perils of pesticides, educating the public about organic agriculture, and calling upon the federal government to regulate the use of the term to ensure strict standards customers could trust.

For years he and like-minded advocates lobbied for the USDA to create standards governing organic certification, so that Americans anywhere could see that word and know what they were eating was grown without synthetic fertilizers, pesticides, herbicides, or fungicides. And their work finally paid off—in the final months of the Clinton administration, the USDA moved ahead to create a National Organic Program (NOP) regulating certification.

But as Otto von Bismarck famously wrote, to see laws or sausage being made is to lose respect for either. Indeed, John watched in horror as industrial-ag conglomerates had their way in Washington. And when the ink was dry on the NOP, a full 142 synthetic chemicals, from tetracycline to stretramyalin, were allowed in agricultural products bearing the O-word.

"It was like my world came crashing down," says John.

He had lobbied for years for this very law, and was devastated to see exceptions for chemicals that, in his words, "are so destructive to the environment they shouldn't even be allowed in conventional agriculture, let alone organic." (Allowing those 142 chemicals, by the way, is just one of sixty-three issues to which farmers like John so ardently object.) As he saw it, the certification he'd dedicated much of his life to building was now so lax that it was effectively meaningless.

It took almost a year to come to grips with, but after twenty years of being certified organic by the state, the Gorzynski family decided to give up the term rather than participate in a certification they could no longer stand by. Still, while so many organic brands are owned by Dean Foods, General Mills, Hershey, Con-Agra, Cargill, Pepsi, and Hain-Celestial, John still believes in the kind of agriculture for which he no longer has an easy adjective. And while he's legally not allowed to answer in the affirmative when customers ask if his farm is organic, he finds that most are more than happy with his complicated answer.

(continued) ▶

"I explain that I was certified for twenty years and that organic certification now allows 142 synthetics, and I don't use any of them. That I don't own a spray rig. And that my farm uses nothing but seeds, sun, soil, and water."

And in the end, most customers come to realize that the one word they were looking for is actually an inadequate stand-in for exactly what they get at the market—the chance to meet the farmers themselves and have a face-to-face conversation about how their food is grown.

It's clear that John's customers value his honest food more than any federal certification. When his not-organic farm suffered floods, this concerned community ponied up donations, even demanded that he raise prices. After thirty years selling at Union Square, he sees not only his customers' kids growing up, but now grandkids too. And customers who have moved away still visit when they're passing through New York, showing pictures of their families and asking after his.

His crops have grown up too. When he first came to Greenmarket back in 1979, customers had never seen sugar snap peas, delicata squash, or a head of red lettuce. "People were like, 'Oh my God, what *is* that?'" laughs John. "Their base of food knowledge was so limited. But today it's grown beyond anybody's expectations. Within a lifetime to see the number of wild foods available—purslane, dandelion, calalloo, nettles, lambs quarters. When I first started, all the other farmers would make fun of me for the weeds on my table. But the nutrients in those wild things are so superior, up to nine times the nutrients of cultivated crops. To have helped widen horizons so much within my lifetime is wonderful."

He now grows about 600 varieties of vegetables and 300 of fruit—including well over 100 varieties of lettuce alone. And he saves the seeds for many crops crossed right on his farm: parsnips, burdock, mustard greens, spinach, beets, and a particular leek he's been saving for decades. And while his apples next to shiny supermarket specimens look like a seasoned boxer alongside a made-up model, John says he's growing for flavor, not cosmetics. "They look like apples are supposed to look, and they taste like apples are supposed to taste."

Still, there's the semantic matter of how to describe the way he farms. He sometimes uses terms such as permaculture or nutrient dense or petrochemical-free. But back in 2000 when the family decided to drop certification, John's wife's license plate read "GO Farm," an exhortation that riffed on the name Gorzynski Organic Farm. "We needed another O word," John says. They landed on one that felt exactly right.

"'Ornery' was just so easy. It was exactly how I felt about the government grab. And I continue to be ornery to this day when it comes to that. But otherwise I enjoy life. Ninety percent of my crops are thriving. The word 'organic' in this country is greatly diminished. But I continue to stand here and be ornery and do what I do, which I'm proud of."

GRILLED PEACHES AND ROMANESCO SQUASH WITH GRAINS AND TOMATO

By **LIVIO VELARDO, GOTHAM BAR AND GRILL**

These days, it seems like every young culinary school graduate has a turnip tattoo and a farm-to-table business plan. But Gotham Bar and Grill's Chef Portale has been building his menus out of Union Square bounty for thirty years—longer than many of those cooks have been eating solid food.

This dish takes a little work—cooking the grains, then grilling the squash and peaches in batches—but the fantastically flavorful results are well worth the effort. Speaking of "worth it," Romanesco squash—an Italian heirloom variety of summer squash with pretty gray flecks and prominent ribs—typically costs more than garden-variety zucchini because the plant yields only half as much as hybrids, which it more than makes up for with its wonderfully nutty flavor.

Bring a medium saucepan full of water to a boil and season with salt. Add the bulgur wheat and boil, similar to the way you cook pasta, until tender, 10 to 12 minutes, and drain well through a fine mesh strainer. Transfer to a mixing bowl and toss with the lemon juice and 1 tablespoon of olive oil.

In a small mixing bowl, combine the mustard, white balsamic, and salt and pepper to taste. While whisking, slowly add ⅓ cup of olive oil to make a vinaigrette. Set aside.

Slice each peach into 12 wedges. In a large bowl, combine the peaches with the squash and toss with 2 tablespoons of olive oil, plus salt and pepper to taste.

Preheat a grill or grill pan over medium-high heat.

Working in batches, grill the squash about 2 minutes per side, then the peach wedges, about 1 minute per side. Remove from the grill and return to the same bowl. Add the tomato, red onion, and basil.

To serve, spread the bulgur wheat on a serving platter. Top with the squash-peach-tomato mixture and dress with the vinaigrette.

1 CUP BULGUR WHEAT

1 TABLESPOON LEMON JUICE, FROM ABOUT ½ A LEMON

½ CUP EXTRA VIRGIN OLIVE OIL, DIVIDED

1 TEASPOON DIJON MUSTARD

3 TABLESPOONS WHITE BALSAMIC VINEGAR

SALT AND FRESHLY GROUND BLACK PEPPER

2 RIPE PEACHES

2 ROMANESCO SQUASH, SLICED INTO ½-INCH ROUNDS

1 LARGE HEIRLOOM OR BEEFSTEAK TOMATO, SLICED INTO ½-INCH WEDGES

½ THINLY SLICED RED ONION

¼ CUP GENTLY PACKED BASIL LEAVES

PAN ROASTED SWORDFISH WITH EGGPLANT "CAVIAR" AND TEARDROP TOMATO SALAD

by **GABRIEL KREUTHER**

Eggplant Caviar

1 POUND EGGPLANT, ABOUT
2 SMALL

1 MEDIUM WHITE ONION, PEELED
AND CUT IN HALF

2 TABLESPOONS OLIVE OIL

1 FINELY CHOPPED GARLIC CLOVE

1 TABLESPOON CHOPPED
FLAT-LEAF PARSLEY

2 TEASPOONS SHERRY VINEGAR

1 PINCH ALEPPO PEPPER
(OPTIONAL)

SALT AND FRESHLY GROUND
BLACK PEPPER TO TASTE

Teardrop Tomato Salad

6 OUNCES MIXED TEARDROP
OR CHERRY TOMATOES,
CUT IN HALF

1 TABLESPOON LEMON JUICE,
FROM ABOUT ½ OF A LEMON

1 TABLESPOON EXTRA VIRGIN
OLIVE OIL

2 CUPS BABY ARUGULA, WASHED

SALT AND FRESHLY GROUND
BLACK PEPPER TO TASTE

This apex predator can grow up to ten feet long and is one of the fastest fish in the sea. While swordfish's delicious meat has been prized since ancient times, the species was so overfished in recent decades, it almost became the one that got away. But this fish tale has a happy ending—swordfish stocks rebounded, and today the North Atlantic population is well worth hooking and cooking.

This dish includes three components, but each is simple enough for a quick weeknight dinner that tastes like four-star preparation. The pale pink flesh eats like steak—if tuna is the chicken of the sea, swordfish is the ocean's filet mignon.

Preheat the oven to 400° F.

Prepare the eggplant: Halve the eggplants and with the tip of a paring knife, cut crosswise slices into the flesh, about ½-inch deep. Season the eggplants and the onion with salt and pepper, drizzle with the olive oil, and place face down on a baking sheet. Roast for 30 minutes or until they begin to collapse when tapped. Remove from the oven, scoop the flesh from the eggplants, and let them drain in a colander for 15 to 20 minutes. Meanwhile, finely chop the onion. Transfer the eggplant flesh to a bowl, mix in the onion, garlic, parsley, sherry vinegar, and season with the salt, pepper, and Aleppo pepper. Set aside at room temperature if eating within an hour; otherwise, refrigerate.

Make the tomato salad: Toss the tomatoes, lemon juice, and olive oil gently in a bowl. Just before serving, add the arugula and season with salt and pepper.

Prepare the swordfish: Pat the fish dry and season both sides with salt and pepper. Heat a 12-inch sauté pan over medium-high heat, coat with the grapeseed oil, reduce heat to medium, and sear the fish to desired doneness, about 2 minutes per side. Serve immediately, atop eggplant caviar, with salad alongside and finished with an extra drizzle of olive oil.

SERVES 4

Swordfish

1 POUND SWORDFISH, ABOUT 1-INCH THICK, SKIN REMOVED AND CUT INTO 4 PORTIONS

SALT AND FRESHLY GROUND BLACK PEPPER

1 TABLESPOON GRAPESEED OIL (OR OLIVE OIL)

NO-BAKE GOAT CHEESE CHEESECAKE WITH NECTARINE COMPOTE

by **LOUISA SHAFIA, AUTHOR OF** *THE NEW PERSIAN KITCHEN*

If you were to list the qualities of an ideal summer dessert, you'd find this cheesecake has them all. It uses neither oven nor stove. It's completely make-ahead: spin the crust together in a food processor, press it into a springform pan, whip the filling, and toss it in the fridge. Its flavors are simultaneously simple and surprising, giving a tangy twist to classic cheesecake. Don't be cowed by the use of goat cheese—even skeptics will lick their forks clean.

Perhaps best of all, while this cheesecake is great straight, it's also the perfect platform for whatever fruit catches your eye at the market, be they gooseberries or apricots.

Lightly grease a 10-inch springform pan.

Prepare the cheesecake: In a food processor, combine the pistachios and graham crackers with the melted butter, cinnamon, and 2 tablespoons of sugar. Add a pinch of salt and pulse until the mixture has a sandy texture and starts to form clumps, about 30 seconds to 1 minute. Transfer to the springform pan and spread evenly over the bottom. Press down with the bottom of a juice glass to pack it evenly.

In the bowl of an electric mixer fitted with the whisk attachment, whip the cream into stiff peaks. Transfer the whipped cream to a bowl and set aside. Replace the mixer bowl without washing.

Cheesecake

1½ CUPS TOASTED PISTACHIOS

1 CUP CRUSHED GRAHAM CRACKERS, FROM ABOUT 7 TO 8 LARGE GRAHAM CRACKERS

4 TABLESPOONS MELTED, UNSALTED BUTTER (PLUS MORE FOR GREASING PAN)

½ TEASPOON GROUND CINNAMON

1 CUP PLUS 2 TABLESPOONS SUGAR, DIVIDED

SALT

½ CUP HEAVY CREAM

1 POUND FRESH, CRUMBLED GOAT CHEESE, AT ROOM TEMPERATURE

¾ CUP CRÈME FRAÎCHE

1 TABLESPOON LIME JUICE, FROM ABOUT 1 LIME

Nectarine Compote

2 RIPE NECTARINES, CUT INTO WEDGES

2 TABLESPOONS SUGAR

1 TABLESPOON LIME JUICE, FROM ABOUT 1 LIME

(continued) ▶

Combine the goat cheese, crème fraîche, and 1 cup of sugar in the bowl of the mixer fitted with the whisk attachment and beat for 2 to 3 minutes, until smooth. Add the lime juice and a pinch of salt and fold in the whipped cream. Pour the mixture into the springform pan and smooth the top. Chill in the refrigerator for at least 4 hours, or until firm.

Meanwhile make the compote: Mix the nectarines with the sugar and lime juice and let sit at room temperature for about 30 minutes to 1 hour.

Serve the cheesecake with compote over the top. The cheesecake will keep in the refrigerator for up to 4 days.

MAKES ONE 10-INCH CAKE, SERVING 8 TO 10

BLUEBERRY GOOSEBERRY CROSTATA

by **PETER HOFFMAN, BACK FORTY AND BACK FORTY WEST**

A crostata is simply a rustic fruit tart with free-form edges, rather than a pie plate, holding in the fruit. They're common in Italy, and here Chef Hoffman spikes his dough with semolina flour, which gives the crust something of a sconelike crumb.

When working with the dough, don't rush your roll—it's important to get it good and thin—but feel free to improvise on the fruit—you can use four cups of whatever inspires you. Here Chef Hoffman combines blueberries with gooseberries, which are beloved in Europe but little-known stateside; when they first appear at market, gooseberries are firm and somewhat tart, turning sweeter and softer as the weeks go by. Another terrific combination is peaches, apricots, and plums with a sliced yellow tomato in the mix—after all, it's a fruit too!

No matter your fruit filling, this tart is lovely solo, but even better with fresh whipped cream, a scoop of vanilla ice cream, or a dollop of plain, tangy yogurt.

Make the dough: In the bowl of a food processor, combine both flours with the baking powder, sugar, and salt and pulse a few times to combine. Add the diced butter and pulse about ten times, until the butter is cut into pea-sized pieces. Continue to pulse four to five more times as you slowly pour in the eggs and the dough begins to come together.

Turn the dough out onto a lightly floured surface and knead gently, two to three times, until the dough comes together. Press into a disc shape, wrap with plastic, and chill in the refrigerator for at least one hour, or overnight.

Crostata Dough

2 CUPS ALL-PURPOSE FLOUR

1 CUP SEMOLINA FLOUR

1½ TABLESPOONS BAKING POWDER

1 TABLESPOON SUGAR

1 TEASPOON SALT

8 TABLESPOONS DICED COLD BUTTER

3 WHOLE BEATEN EGGS

Fruit Filling

½ CUP SUGAR

3 TABLESPOONS ALL-PURPOSE FLOUR

¼ TEASPOON GROUND CINNAMON

2 CUPS BLUEBERRIES

2 CUPS GOOSEBERRIES, TOPS OFF

ZEST OF 1 LEMON

(continued) ▶

Remove the dough from the fridge and let rest at room temperature to temper, about 10 minutes. Meanwhile, preheat the oven to 400°F and tape a piece of parchment paper to your countertop. Generously flour the parchment and roll the rested dough into a rough circle about ¼-inch thick. Remove the tape and transfer the dough, on the parchment, to a baking sheet. Set aside while you make the filling.

For the filling: In a medium bowl, whisk together the sugar, flour, and cinnamon. Add the berries and lemon zest and stir to combine. Pour the filling into the middle of the rolled-out dough and bring the edges up and over the perimeter, loosely folding and pinching so that the free-form shape holds the fruit inside the tart.

Optional: Brush the exposed dough lightly with milk or egg to give it a little suntan in the oven and/or sprinkle coarse sugar on for a sparkling finish.

Bake for 15 minutes at 400°F, then lower the heat to 375°F and bake for another 20 to 25 minutes or until the crust is golden and the fruit is cooked and bubbly. Allow to cool before serving.

Farmer CHIP KENT
LOCUST GROVE FRUIT FARM

Chip Kent is the sixth generation to run Locust Grove Farm, but he was just fifteen in 1976 when his father took him down to sell apples in the Big Apple for the Greenmarket's experimental, inaugural season.

Back then Union Square was a drug haven known as "Needle Park," but addicts aren't the only thing Chip remembers. "The customers," he recalls, "they loved us. They *loved* us. They were just so glad to be able to buy fresh produce in the city."

These days, Chip laughs, the methadone users now share the park with models, and the nearly empty building that was long home to a bag lady now houses a multilevel Barnes & Noble. But the city isn't the only thing that's changed. The orchard has too—for the better.

Locust Grove was founded in 1820 in a part of Ulster County that's justifiably famous for its fruit; the family farm is just a stone fruit's throw from the dock where the area's apples were long loaded onto barges to feed a growing city. But by the time Chip was a boy, Hudson Valley farms had fallen onto hard times. Most of Locust Grove's fruit was sold at little roadside stands, which were fast losing ground to supermarkets stocked with cheap, shiny fruit from distant lands. Meanwhile American orchards' longstanding biodiversity had suffered what author Michael Pollan calls a brutal winnowing. Locust Grove's own apple crop was down to pretty much just red delicious and Macs.

But once the Kents started selling in the city, they could ignore trends toward industrialization

◀ *Once the Kents started selling in the city, they could ignore trends toward industrialization and instead offer what customers wanted: diversity. Today Locust Grove grows twenty-five types of plums and more varieties of peaches than they can count.* (Amanda Gentile)

and instead listen to what customers wanted: diversity. Today Locust Grove grows twenty-five types of plums, a dozen different pears, seventy varieties of apples, and an entire acre of quince. "I can't tell you how many varieties of peaches," Chip laughs, "but it's a lot."

Many such fruits, such as gooseberries and currants, ripened on these same hills a century ago and suddenly are back in demand. But the Kents also happily plant new varieties that offer great flavor: tangos, yellow donut peaches, and an as-yet unnamed nectarine that customers are already gaga for. Other new strains offer old-fashioned flavor earlier and later—some peach trees, for example, now bear fruit at the beginning of July, while others are ripe for the picking right through the end of September, making summer last a little longer.

The Kents follow a practice called Integrated Pest Management, using careful scouts to track insect populations and applying only minimal treatments at the precise moment of pest reproduction, to save a crop. "We like the good bugs," says Chip, "and we live in the middle of this operation ourselves, so the less we spray, the better."

Chefs swarm their city stands, drawn by the fruit's freshness and the unusual offerings, from Saturn peaches and shiro plums to black raspberries and pink lady apples. These days Chip is often too busy at the farm to drive down and wait on them himself, but old-time shoppers may see what looks like the young man who first sold at market thirty-five years ago: Chip's own son Sawyer is in college, planning to be the seventh generation to run Locust Grove, and Chip has to chuckle when Sawyer and his younger brothers come back from a day in the city with stories of selling at the stand all day. Fortunately today's adventures have little in common with the bad old days—except for customer appreciation. Chip loves hearing Sawyer's report that New Yorkers are hooked on the fruit.

MIDSUMMER FRUIT CLAFOUTIS

by **MARY CLEAVER, THE GREEN TABLE AND THE CLEAVER COMPANY**

Crust

1 CUP ALL-PURPOSE FLOUR

PINCH OF SALT

8 TABLESPOONS COLD UNSALTED BUTTER, CUT INTO PIECES

1 TO 3 TABLESPOONS ICE WATER, DEPENDING ON THE HUMIDITY

Filling

½ CUP HEAVY CREAM (GENEROUS POUR)

¼ CUP FRESH LEMON VERBENA LEAVES (OR 1 TABLESPOON DRIED)

½ CUP SUGAR

2 LARGE BEATEN EGGS

2 TABLESPOONS ALL-PURPOSE FLOUR

Fruit

2 TO 3 CUPS SUMMER FRUIT, ANY COMBINATION OF PITTED CHERRIES, SLICED STONE FRUIT, AND/OR WHOLE BERRIES

Mary Cleaver—who has been building her catering menus around local harvests since the Greenmarket's inception in 1976 and now has her own family farm upstate—says that this dish catches the essence of summer. You can use any and all stone fruits, berries, or currants, and as the season progresses, this dessert becomes more and more colorful: In late June, she makes it with sour cherries, which quickly yield the stage to a more riotous palette and palate of colorful sweet and tangy midsummer fruits.

For the crust: In a medium bowl or the bowl of a food processor, combine the flour and a pinch of salt. Add the butter and, using two knives or a pastry blender, cut the butter into the flour (or process quickly in a food processor) until the mixture resembles coarse meal. Add ice water a tablespoon at a time, fully incorporating into the dough before deciding whether you need to add more. Once the dough comes together, shape it into a ball, flatten, wrap in parchment, and refrigerate until cold.

When chilled, roll the dough out on a hard surface, dusting with flour as needed so it doesn't stick to the rolling surface or pin. Transfer the pastry to a 10-inch tart pan with removable bottom, finishing the top edge evenly with your thumbs. Prick the bottom with a fork and refrigerate for at least 1 hour to rest the dough.

Preheat the oven to 400°F.

To prebake the shell, line it with foil, and fill it with dried beans or other pie weights. Bake in the middle of the oven for 15 minutes, then remove the foil and weights and bake for another 5 or so minutes, until the crust is dry but has not taken on any color. Cool on a wire rack.

(continued) ▶

For the filling: Combine the cream and lemon verbena in a saucepan, bring just to the boiling point and simmer for a minute or so (the cream will thicken a bit), then remove from heat. Cool, then strain through a fine mesh sieve, pressing on the verbena to extract all the cream—you want a full ½ cup of infused cream. Discard the verbena and set the cream aside to cool.

In a medium bowl, mix the sugar and eggs until well combined. Stir in the flour and herb-infused cream.

Assembly: Fill the crust generously with the fruit and pour the custard over, allowing it to distribute evenly and fill in any gaps. If there is any fruit juice left, pour it over the top of the custard. Bake for 30 minutes, until the custard is set and lightly golden. Serve warm. Hopefully you will have some left to refrigerate and eat cold for breakfast.

SERVES 6 TO 8

APRICOT JAM

BETH LINSKEY, BETH'S FARM KITCHEN

La vie est dur sans confiture. That French phrase means "Life is hard without jam," and it is that sentiment on which Beth Linskey's business is based. Spring through fall, she buys peak produce from the farmers around her in the Hudson Valley, simmering the harvest into the likes of damson plum jam, mint jelly, blazing tomato chutney, and dilly pickled carrots.

Fortunately for us, one of her most popular preserves is also one of the simplest to make. Each August when the apricots are ambrosial, buy extra to simmer with sugar and capture summer in a jar.

Remember to stir from the bottom to avoid scorching—a flat-bottom spatula works well for this. If you're feeling ambitious, it's fun to make a bigger batch and seal your jars to keep in the cupboard, but beginners can simply keep the finished jam in the fridge, no boiling water bath needed.

Beth's variation for Neachy-Cot Jam follows: reduce the amount of apricots to ½ cup (from ½ pound whole fruit) and add 2 cups of chopped nectarines (from 1½ pounds whole fruit) and 1⅓ cups chopped peaches (from 1 pound whole fruit). Because peaches and nectarines are juicier than apricots, use only 2½ tablespoons of water for this variation.

Either *confiture* will make your life easier and sweeter.

4 CUPS PITTED APRICOTS, CHOPPED OR MASHED (2 TO 3 POUNDS WHOLE APRICOTS)

2 CUPS SUGAR

In a medium pot, combine the fruit with ½ cup of water and bring to a simmer. Cook until the fruit is the consistency of thick applesauce, about 20 minutes. Add the sugar and continue to cook, uncovered, over medium heat, stirring the bottom of the pot regularly to prevent scorching, for 10 to 15 minutes. Remove from the heat when the jam has thickened and sheets off a spoon. Pour into sterilized jars or refrigerator containers.

MAKES 4 TO 5 8-OUNCE JARS

CANTALOUPE AND HYSSOP POPS

by **PEOPLE'S POPS**

¾ CUP SUGAR (PREFERABLY ORGANIC, RAW SUGAR)

10 SPRIGS HYSSOP

1 SMALL CANTALOUPE, ABOUT 35 OUNCES

A simple syrup infusion of the herb anise hyssop adds a sweet licorice kiss to cantaloupe in these popsicles. A member of the mint family that is named for its anise-evoking aroma, anise hyssop grows wild throughout much of North America, but farmers grow it from seed, using the sweetest and most aromatic cultivars. It is beloved by bees and hummingbirds—and cooks! The longer you steep it, the stronger the flavor.

When selecting your cantaloupe, look for one that feels heavy, gives slightly when you press it gently with your fingers, and smells delicious.

If you don't own popsicle molds, don't get brain freeze. Popsicles can be frozen in small cups of any sort—from shot glasses to Dixie cups. For ease of sliding the pops out of their molds, look for shapes that are somewhat tapered (wider at the end where the stick comes out).

In a medium saucepan combine the sugar with ¾ cup of water and the hyssop. Warm over medium-high heat, whisking gently to dissolve the sugar. Do not boil. Remove from the heat, cover with a lid, and let steep for 30 minutes. Discard the hyssop and cool the syrup to room temperature or in the refrigerator. (The syrup can be prepared a day in advance.)

Peel, seed, and dice the cantaloupe, then puree in a blender until completely smooth. Add the syrup to taste until the mixture tastes quite sweet and the hyssop is detectable. Pour the mixture into your ice pop molds, leaving one-quarter inch of headspace at the top for the expansion that occurs during freezing. After 1 to 2 hours, when the mixture is semi-frozen, insert sticks, then freeze until solid, 4 to 5 hours.

MAKES 10 POPS

SPICY WATERMELON GRANITA

by **FANY GERSON, LA NEWYORKINA**

If you can't stand the heat, get into the kitchen to make this grown-up granita. There's no need for an ice cream maker—simply simmer up a sugar-lime-jalapeño syrup, stir it with pureed watermelon, and freeze it into sweet, spicy slush, stirring and scraping occasionally (a serving fork works well for this). The resulting DIY slushy is simultaneously bracing, sweet, spicy, bright, and undeniably refreshing.

This recipe can easily be doubled, and needless to say, it freezes well. For an extra tongue-tingling finish, mix up a teaspoon of salt with half a teaspoon of chili powder and sprinkle a pinch over each serving.

½ **LIME**

⅓ **CUP SUGAR**

1 **SERRANO OR JALAPEÑO CHILE, SLICED LENGTHWISE**

3 **CUPS (ABOUT 1¼ POUNDS) CUBED AND SEEDED WATERMELON**

½ **TEASPOON SALT**

Peel a few large strips of zest from the lime, then squeeze the juice into a cup and set aside.

In a small saucepan, combine the sugar with ½ cup of water and place over high heat until the mixture comes to a simmer and the sugar dissolves completely. Remove from the heat, add the chile and lime zest, and steep, covered, for 15 minutes.

Meanwhile, puree the watermelon with the salt and lime juice in a blender or food processor and pour into a 9 x 13 inch shallow pan. Strain the syrup into the watermelon puree, stir to combine, and transfer the pan to the freezer.

After 2 hours, scrape the granita mix with a fork (a serving fork works well for this) and return it to the freezer. Freeze until it is firm, about another 3 hours, and when you are ready to serve, take the granita mixture out of the freezer for 5 to 10 minutes and scrape with a fork. Serve in individual cups.

SERVES 4 TO 6

YOGURT GELATO AND PLUM SORBET

by **JON SNYDER, IL LABORATORIO DEL GELATO**

Yogurt Gelato

MAKES 1 PINT

1 CUP HALF AND HALF

4 TABLESPOONS SUGAR

1 TEASPOON PEACH OR APRICOT JAM (SEE BETH'S FARM KITCHEN RECIPE, PAGE 119)

1 CUP LOW FAT OR NONFAT YOGURT

Plum Sorbet

MAKES 1 PINT

7 TO 8 BLACK PLUMS (OTHER VARIETIES CAN BE USED), ENOUGH TO YIELD 12 OUNCES OF PUREE

4 TABLESPOONS SUGAR

When it comes to great cooking, ingredients are far more important than equipment. But while you don't need a tricked-out kitchen to eat very, very well, an ice cream maker is an awful lot of fun—and an easy way to enjoy fresh flavors long past their harvest season.

The produce-driven possibilities for ice cream are endless, as evidenced by Jon Snyder's two hundred market-driven seasonal flavors from basil to Braeburn, but these two recipes are child's play, each taking only a few minutes to put together. The yields are small—only a few scoops each—because Snyder says small batches are far smoother. "I always recommend filling a home machine half full," he writes, "because overfilling or even filling the contents will raise the temperature, and for the best final result, you want a *very* cold machine. This helps tremendously with texture." That said, if you want to double these batches, we won't tell.

For yogurt gelato: In a small pan, combine the half and half, sugar, and preserves and simmer over low heat until hot but not boiling. Strain to remove preserves. Chill until very cold, the colder the better—overnight or at least 8 hours is highly recommended. Combine with the yogurt and mix well, but do not overblend. Pour into a well-chilled ice cream machine. Churn, freeze, and enjoy.

For plum sorbet: Pit the plums and puree in a blender or food processor. The skin will get incorporated and diffuse into the pulp to create a rich, beautiful color. Don't process fully—the small skin bits add a nice contrast. Add the sugar and 4 tablespoons of water. Stir well and refrigerate for at least 1 hour. Pour into an ice cream machine. Churn, freeze, and enjoy.

OYAMEL MARASCHINO CHERRIES

by **JOSÉ ANDRÉS, CHEF/OWNER OF THINKFOODGROUP**

Forget the lurid food dye—maraschino cherries are not a factory invention. And making your own is a snap.

Get ready in late June by securing a bottle of maraschino liqueur, then ask the fruit farmers how the cherry harvest is coming along. Sweet cherries come in first, but bide your time—sours arrive around the Fourth of July, when they're traditionally baked into pie. Instead of rolling out dough, simply simmer up this syrup and stockpile the results for homemade Manhattans.

This oft-overlooked fruit is good for more than just garnet garnishes. While many Americans are scared off by their name, so-called sour cherries contain flavors Jolly Rancher can never imitate. And it's easy to take advantage of their short season. Simply cook them up with a few spoonfuls of sugar for the best ice cream topping you've ever tasted.

1 POUND SOUR CHERRIES

½ CUP SUGAR

1 TABLESPOON LEMON JUICE

¼-INCH CINNAMON STICK

¼ VANILLA BEAN

1 CUP MARASCHINO LIQUEUR

¼ CUP XTABENTUN LIQUEUR (OPTIONAL)

Pit the cherries and set aside.

Combine all other ingredients in a large saucepot with ½ cup of water and bring to a simmer.

Stir until the sugar is dissolved, about 5 minutes. Add the cherries and remove from heat. Allow the cherries to steep in the liquid until they reach room temperature. Transfer to a jar and cover. Store them in the refrigerator in their cooking liquid. They will last forever.

CORN GODDESS

by **DAVID WONDRICH**

This cocktail takes advantage of the sweetness of late summer corn and cherry tomatoes to make for a drink that's silky and intriguing. Be sure to muddle well to extract produce juices before straining.

To double strain, use a Hawthorne strainer (the one with the spring) in the mixing tin as one normally would, but rest a julep strainer (the one that's like a perforated spoon) over the glass to catch the corn and tomato pulp and tomato seeds.

Each sip starts out barely sweet but ends with Campari's bitter finish, leading you back for another mouthful, and another.

4 TABLESPOONS FRESH CORN KERNELS, OR ½ OUNCE FRESHLY MADE CORN JUICE

2 HALVED CHERRY TOMATOES

1 OUNCE FORD'S OR PLYMOUTH GIN

1 OUNCE CAMPARI

1 FRESH SAGE LEAF

Muddle in a cocktail shaker the corn, tomatoes, and gin. Add the Campari. Shake well with ice and double strain into chilled cocktail glass; float a sage leaf on top as garnish.

MAKES 1 COCKTAIL

LUCAMANNO FREDDO CUCUMBER COCKTAIL

by **JOE CAMPANALE, DELL'ANIMA**

5 MINT LEAVES, PLUS ONE SPRIG FOR GARNISH

6 CUCUMBER SLICES, EACH ABOUT ¼-INCH THICK, PLUS ONE LONG PIECE FOR GARNISH

4½ TABLESPOONS DILL-INFUSED VODKA (SEE HEADNOTE)

1½ TABLESPOONS MINT-INFUSED SIMPLE SYRUP (SEE HEADNOTE)

1½ TABLESPOONS LIME JUICE

A cucumber salad's cocktail cousin, this herbaceous mixed drink calls for two DIY elixirs—dill-infused vodka and mint simple syrup—each of which can be made ahead, by the tablespoon or gallon, depending on how many guests you're expecting. The drink is spectacularly refreshing so you may want to err on the side of extra. But if you run out of supplies, just substitute plain vodka and simple syrup. The cucumber and fresh mint are the stars, and when you see them floating amid the ice, this glass of booze feels as virtuous as taking your vitamins.

To make dill-infused vodka, simply steep a few sprigs of fresh dill in vodka at room temperature for 36 to 48 hours, then strain out the herbs. Joe infuses an entire bottle of vodka at a time, but you can make any amount, and it keeps indefinitely. Nine tablespoons—just more than half a cup—makes enough for two cocktails.

To make mint-infused simple syrup, heat equal parts water and sugar until the sugar is dissolved. Then remove from heat, add a few sprigs of mint, and steep, covered, for 15 minutes, before removing the mint. Like the vodka, you can make any amount, and this keeps in the fridge indefinitely. We suggest a minimum of ½ cup of sugar to ½ cup of water, so you'll have enough liquid in which to submerge the mint.

Muddle the mint and cucumber slices in a rocks glass. Add ice, top with the dill-infused vodka, mint syrup, and lime juice, and stir. Garnish with a sprig of fresh mint and a long slice of fresh cucumber.

MAKES 1 COCKTAIL

Fall

GRILLED ESCAROLE WITH SAUERKRAUT DRESSING

by **DANIEL BOULUD, DBGB KITCHEN AND BAR**

Sauerkraut Dressing

1 CUP DRAINED SAUERKRAUT

2 EGG YOLKS

⅔ CUP EXTRA VIRGIN OLIVE OIL

SALT AND FRESHLY GROUND
WHITE PEPPER

Chile Oil

½ JALAPEÑO, OR 1 TEASPOON
CRUSHED RED PEPPER

⅓ CUP OLIVE OIL

Escarole

2 LARGE HEADS ESCAROLE

SALT AND FRESHLY GROUND
WHITE PEPPER

4 SPRIGS TARRAGON, STEMS
REMOVED AND LEAVES ROUGHLY
CHOPPED (OPTIONAL)

⅓ CUP TOASTED PINE NUTS
(OPTIONAL)

A lettuce look-alike, escarole is actually in the chicory family and thus a cousin of endive, radicchio, and frisée. At their peak in fall, chicories are prized for their slight bitterness and sturdy texture, wonderful in salads and also in cooked preparations like soup and braises. Here Chef Boulud quickly sears quartered escarole in a grill pan and tops it with a creamy dressing that harnesses sauerkraut's bright acidity. Yes, this dressing calls for raw yolks, so use fresh eggs from pastured hens, unmistakable for their deep marigold orange.

Perhaps the best part of this recipe is the chile-infused oil. It couldn't be easier to make—just toss some rough chopped jalapeño or other pepper into oil and bring to a simmer. Make extra—it keeps in the fridge for a month, and you'll find yourself using it to cook everything from omelets to fish.

Make the dressing: In a blender, puree the sauerkraut, egg yolks, and ¼ cup of water until smooth. With the blender running on low, stream in the olive oil until well emulsified. Adjust with salt and pepper to taste.

Infuse the oil: In a small saucepan, combine the jalapeño or crushed red pepper and olive oil over medium heat. Once the oil starts to bubble, remove from the heat, cover, and set aside to infuse for 20 minutes, then strain.

Quarter the escarole heads, leaving stems intact, and run cold water between each leaf to remove any soil; pat dry. Transfer to a large bowl. Drizzle the infused oil over the escarole and sprinkle with salt and pepper. Toss to coat. Marinate for 30 minutes.

Preheat a grill pan or large sauté pan over high heat. In two batches, grill the escarole on all sides until lightly charred and warmed through. Trim the cores. To serve, place 2 quarters on a plate, drizzle generously with dressing, and, if using, sprinkle with tarragon leaves and pine nuts.

SERVES 4

KALE SALAD WITH SERRANO PEPPER AND MINT

by **CHRIS BEISCHER, MERCER KITCHEN**

If you had bought stock in kale salad around 2006, everyone would have called you crazy—and you'd now be sitting pretty. But rather than mull over your missed millions, go out and buy the ingredients to make this salad. They cost only a few bucks, and you'll eat like a mogul.

This salad's flavors are as big as its nutritional cred. It packs heat from the chile, coolness from the mint, lemon juice's bright acidity, and the umami of both anchovy and Parmesan. The avocado and pumpkin seeds are optional but elevate the dish to blue-chip status.

Zest one of the lemons and set aside. Juice both lemons; you should have ¼ cup juice.

In a large bowl, whisk together the lemon juice, red wine vinegar, garlic, anchovy, mustard, egg yolk, salt, and black pepper. In a steady stream, slowly add the olive oil to the bowl while whisking. Add the Parmesan and whisk to thicken.

Remove and discard the kale's stems and thick center ribs, and slice the leaves very thinly crosswise. Add the kale, mint, and chile to the bowl and toss to combine. Let marinate for 5 minutes. Add the avocado, if using, toss gently, and season to taste. Top with toasted pumpkin seeds, if using, and serve.

SERVES 4

2 LEMONS

1 TABLESPOON RED WINE VINEGAR

½ SMALL GARLIC CLOVE, FINELY MINCED

1 ANCHOVY, PACKED IN OLIVE OIL

1 TEASPOON DIJON MUSTARD

1 EGG YOLK

1 TEASPOON SALT

½ TEASPOON BLACK PEPPER

½ CUP EXTRA VIRGIN OLIVE OIL

1 CUP FINELY GRATED PARMESAN

1 BUNCH CURLY KALE, ABOUT 12 OUNCES

½ CUP ROUGHLY CHOPPED MINT LEAVES

1 THINLY SLICED SERRANO CHILE

1 AVOCADO, PITTED, PEELED AND ROUGHLY CHOPPED (OPTIONAL)

⅓ CUP TOASTED PUMPKIN OR WINTER SQUASH SEEDS (TO LEARN HOW TO ROAST SEEDS, SEE PAGE 166)

Farmers KEN AND EILEEN FARNAN

BUZZARD CREST VINEYARDS

Never mind Labor Day or leaf peeping. In late August the unassailable end of summer is announced by a ringing phone: It's Ken and Eileen Farnan of Buzzard Crest Vineyards, calling to say the grapes are ripe and they're ready to come back to market.

A few other Greenmarket farmers grow grapes, lining up quarts alongside their apples and pears, but the Farnan family's annual offerings—more than a dozen varieties, all certified organic—put them in a class all by themselves. Their return each September is the bittersweet signal that soon frost will strike, dusk will fall early, and we'll all be simmering soups and roasting roots. But first, we feast on the fruit of the vine.

The Farnans' fame stems mainly from the varieties they grow, which make you realize the Thompson Seedless in most supermarkets taste like the page these words are printed on. Ken and Eileen, on the other hand, tend vines with names like Marquis, Canadice, Diamond, and Isabella, carrying within their skins off-the-charts flavor.

That's because when corporate chemists were cooking up artificial flavors a few decades ago, they imitated the flavor of real grapes. Meanwhile, other men in lab coats were breeding the flavor right out of the crop, trading it in a Faustian bargain for high yield and long shelf life. As a result, when twenty-first-century eaters taste their first Concord, the flavor is familiar—but only from Magic Markers and Hubba Bubba chewing gum. At Buzzard Crest's stand, the record is set straight. Especially when it comes to their intense grape juice, which contains exactly one ingredient and has no rival in the supermarket aisle or anywhere else.

But beyond their long-prized genes, Buzzard Crest grapes' flavors have another secret ingredient: terroir. The deep, glacial Finger Lakes delay frost and create conditions ideal for grapes. The Farnans' vines grow on a sun-soaked, west-facing slope that overlooks Keuka Lake. Those chemists could not have engineered better conditions.

Their return each September is the bittersweet signal that soon frost will strike, dusk will fall early, and we'll all be simmering soups and roasting roots.

The Farnans had sold their harvests wholesale until a corporate takeover caused the bottom to fall out of the market in 1986. They were considering selling the farm when Ken's mom mailed them a newspaper clipping about the Greenmarket. Almost thirty years later, each Friday night in fall, Ken and Eileen leave the farm loaded with grapes just after midnight, pulling up at Union Square by 5:30 a.m. They'll sell for twelve hours straight before starting the five-hour drive home.

It's a long day but more than worth it, thanks to the kind of customer devotion evidenced by another phone call that came in to the Greenmarket office one summer. It was a woman who had moved from New York to New Mexico and was planning to fly home. Before buying her airline tickets, she wanted to know when Buzzard Crest was expected back at the market.

MARS

CONCORD

MARQUIS

JUPITER

NIAGARA

CACO

CAULIFLOWER AND BEETS WITH SAUCE GRIBICHE

by **MICHAEL POLLAN,**
AUTHOR OF *COOKED: A NATURAL HISTORY OF TRANSFORMATION*

1 POUND GOLDEN BEETS, ABOUT
4 MEDIUM BEETS

KOSHER SALT

2 EGGS

1 HEAD CAULIFLOWER, CUT INTO
BITE-SIZE FLORETS, ABOUT 6 CUPS

2 LARGE LEEKS, WHITE AND LIGHT
GREEN PARTS ONLY, THICKLY
SLICED, ABOUT 3 CUPS

½ CUP EXTRA VIRGIN OLIVE OIL

⅓ CUP CHOPPED FLAT-LEAF
PARSLEY

2 TABLESPOONS BRINED CAPERS,
DRAINED AND ROUGHLY CHOPPED

2 TABLESPOONS FINELY CHOPPED
CORNICHONS

ZEST AND JUICE OF 1 LEMON

¾ TEASPOON SALT

¼ TEASPOON GROUND BLACK
PEPPER

1 FINELY MINCED GARLIC CLOVE

Michael Pollan wisely exhorts us to "eat food, not too much, mostly plants"—easy advice to follow with recipes like this one. Here he bakes beets and blanches cauliflower and leeks, then drizzles it all with a zippy dressing that features capers and cornichons.

Young leeks appear at the markets in spring, but they're at their best in fall, when months of mulching yield more than a foot of the prized stalk. Dark green tops can be saved in the freezer for making stock.

Hidden within this recipe is the perfect method for hard-boiled eggs. Chilling them quickly in ice water yields bright orange yolks.

Blood-red beets may turn the cauliflower and leeks purple, but golden beets won't. Candy-striped Chioggia beets, once cooked, are pale pink.

Preheat the oven to 350°F.

Arrange the beets in a shallow baking dish and add water to reach a depth of ½ inch. Cover the dish tightly with foil and bake the beets until a knife slips in easily, about 1½ hours. When cool enough to handle, peel (skins should slip off easily) and slice into wedges.

Meanwhile, bring a large pot of generously salted water to a boil, and prepare a medium bowl of ice water. Add the eggs to the pot, reduce heat to a simmer, and cook for 11 minutes. Remove the eggs with a slotted spoon and submerge in the ice water to quickly chill. Return the water to a boil then add the cauliflower and cook until just tender, 4 to 5 minutes. Using a slotted spoon, transfer the cauliflower to a colander and rinse with cold water until cool. Drain, dry well, and transfer to a large bowl. Return the water to a boil and repeat the process with the leeks, cooking for about 2 minutes, or until tender.

Once the eggs have cooled, peel and halve them and remove the yolks. Finely chop the whites. In a medium bowl, mash the yolks and whisk with the olive oil until well combined. Then add the finely chopped egg whites, parsley, capers, cornichons, lemon zest and juice, salt, pepper, and garlic to make a dressing.

Arrange the beets on a large serving platter and drizzle 3 tablespoons of dressing on top. Toss the cauliflower and leeks with the remaining dressing and additional salt and pepper to taste, and scatter over the beets. Serve at room temperature.

SERVES 6

BRUSSELS SPROUTS SALAD

by **JONATHAN WAXMAN, BARBUTO**

The words "raw Brussels sprouts" may not set you to salivating, but after one bite of this surprising dish, you'll want to make it again and again. While Brussels sprouts are often paired with hot bacon (such as in Sara Jenkins's habit-forming pasta on page 167), here Chef Waxman serves cabbage's little cousin in a light, lemony slaw that's further brightened by a pretty, pickled red onion. The fresh flavors and gorgeous color make this simple dish a great one to entertain with. At market, ask the farmer whether their fields have had frost yet—nights below freezing wipe out tender crops but make Brussels sprouts even sweeter.

¼ OF A DAY-OLD BAGUETTE (ABOUT A 6- TO 8-INCH PIECE)

6 TABLESPOONS EXTRA VIRGIN OLIVE OIL, DIVIDED

3 GARLIC CLOVES, DIVIDED

1 PURPLE TORPEDO ONION OR SMALL RED ONION

4 TABLESPOONS LEMON JUICE, FROM 2 LEMONS

16 OUNCES BRUSSELS SPROUTS, ABOUT A DOZEN BRUSSELS SPROUTS

½ CUP LOOSELY PACKED FLAT-LEAF PARSLEY

2 OUNCES SHAVED PARMESAN (OPTIONAL)

SALT AND FRESHLY GROUND BLACK PEPPER

Preheat the oven to 375°F.

Slice the baguette in half lengthwise. Open up and drizzle the cut sides with 2 tablespoons of olive oil. Season with salt and pepper and bake until golden, about 10 to 12 minutes. Remove from the oven and rub immediately with 1 cut clove of garlic. Once cool, tear it into bite-sized pieces and add to a large mixing bowl.

Peel and halve the onion, then slice it into ¼-inch thick slices. Peel and smash the remaining 2 garlic cloves.

Heat a medium sauté pan over medium heat. Add 1 tablespoon of olive oil, then the onions and garlic. Season with ½ teaspoon of salt and a few cranks of black pepper and cook slowly over low heat until tender, 10 to 12 minutes. Remove the pan from the heat, remove the garlic cloves, and add the lemon juice and 3 tablespoons of olive oil. Let rest in the sauté pan.

Trim the cut end of the sprouts. Using a mandoline or a sharp knife, slice the sprouts lengthwise as thin as possible. Add to the large mixing bowl. Pour the onion mixture over top and toss well to combine.

Finish with the parsley leaves and Parmesan. Adjust the salt, pepper, and lemon juice to taste and serve.

SERVES 3 TO 4

FALL ROASTED VEGETABLES AND FRUITS WITH PECORINO AND WALNUT VINAIGRETTE

by **CEDRIC VONGERICHTEN, PERRY STREET**

Fall Vegetables

2½ POUNDS MIXED ROOT VEGETABLES, INCLUDING PARSNIPS, CARROTS, SWEET POTATOES, JERUSALEM ARTICHOKES, AND CELERIAC

3 TABLESPOONS OLIVE OIL

2 TEASPOONS SALT

BLACK PEPPER

Walnut Vinaigrette

3 TABLESPOONS APPLE CIDER VINEGAR

2 TABLESPOONS WALNUT OIL (OR OLIVE OIL)

2 TABLESPOONS EXTRA VIRGIN OLIVE OIL

SALT AND PEPPER TO TASTE

To Finish

1 APPLE, QUARTERED, CORE REMOVED, SLICED THINLY CROSSWISE

1 CUP CONCORD GRAPES, HALVED AND SEEDS REMOVED, ABOUT 6 OUNCES

½ CUP TOASTED WALNUTS (OR PECANS, ALMONDS, PISTACHIOS, PINE NUTS)

2 OUNCES PECORINO CHEESE

½ CUP BUCKWHEAT SPROUTS (OPTIONAL)

While all Americans know carrots and sweet potatoes, many are unfamiliar with celeriac. Sometimes as large as a softball, the knobby vegetable is also known as celery root and is often sold with a few small celery stalks still attached. Cut off the bumpy skin with a chef's knife and save it for stock; the inner flesh is like a perfumed potato. The French eat it grated raw in a rémoulade, but it's wonderful simmered into soups or in a rich mash; here, a simple roasting concentrates its sweetness, alongside a cornucopia of other roots and tubers.

Concord grapes also appear at market in September, and if you're used to supermarket Thompson seedless, you might want to sit down before trying them. Yes, Concords have thicker skins and contain seeds, but the taste is worth the trouble. Artificial grape flavor was based on this variety before it disappeared from countertops, so customers familiar with cough syrup have been known to exclaim, "It tastes like purple!"

Preheat the oven to 425°F.

Peel the sweet potatoes or celeriac, if using, and cut all the vegetables into 1-inch pieces. Spread on a sheet pan and toss with the olive oil, salt, and pepper. Roast for 35 to 45 minutes, stirring once, until lightly caramelized and tender.

While the vegetables roast, whisk together the apple cider vinegar, walnut oil (if using), and olive oil and season with salt and pepper to taste.

When the vegetables have cooled slightly, transfer them to a large bowl and add the apple, grapes, and toasted walnuts. Toss with the dressing and season to taste. Garnish with shaved Pecorino cheese and buckwheat sprouts.

SERVES 4

FENNEL SALAD WITH GOAT CHEESE AND HAZELNUTS

by **APRIL BLOOMFIELD, THE SPOTTED PIG AND AUTHOR OF** *A GIRL AND HER PIG*

Fennel may be less well known in the States than its cousins—carrots, parsley, or dill—but as with those fellow members of the Umbelliferae family, it has hollow stems, forms a beautiful "umbel" seed head, and is prized in European farmhouse kitchens. Fennel can grow to be several feet tall and serves multiple culinary purposes—the seeds and small flowers (often mislabeled pollen) are anise-y spices; the frilly, dill-like leaves can be used as a fresh herb or garnish; and the green stalks are aromatic in soup stock. But the plant is best known for the large, white, barely sweet bulb at its base, which can be eaten raw or cooked. Here Chef Bloomfield prepares it both ways in a single dish.

She writes, "The crunch of the raw fennel is great in contrast with the creaminess of its roasted counterpart, and the tangy goat cheese gives it complexity and richness. The little bit of chile and the spicy greens will add a nice bit of heat to balance it all out."

Fennel is especially refreshing in the cold months when lettuces have taken their annual bow. In many kitchens at that time, seasonal apples share fruit bowls with various citrus from farther afield. In this dish, feel free to substitute blood oranges for a slight bitterness, mandarins for extra sweetness, or tangelos, which carry a touch of tartness. Taste the vinaigrette, which can be made well in advance, and adjust it for acidity according to which citrus you use.

Preheat the oven to 350°F.

To prepare the citrus: Zest both oranges and set zest aside. Next, "supreme" the oranges: cut the ends off and then carefully cut away the remaining peel, removing all of the bitter white pith. Next, using a sawing motion, cut out each individual segment from the orange. Set the core aside and place the segments in the fridge to chill.

For the Citrus

2 LARGE NAVEL ORANGES

1 JUICED LEMON

2 TEASPOONS SEA SALT

½ CUP EXTRA VIRGIN OLIVE OIL

For the Fennel

4 LARGE BULBS OF FENNEL WITH TOPS

¼ CUP PLUS 1 TABLESPOON EXTRA VIRGIN OLIVE OIL

1 TEASPOON KOSHER SALT

1 TEASPOON CRUSHED DRY PEQUIN CHILE OR RED PEPPER FLAKES

1 LEMON

For the Plate

5 OUNCES CREAMY GOATS' CHEESE

4 CUPS SPICY MARKET GREENS (FRESH ROCKET, WILD WATERCRESS, OR BABY MUSTARD GREENS)

1 SMALL HANDFUL HAZELNUTS, TOASTED AND LIGHTLY CRUSHED

SEA SALT TO TASTE

LEMON TO TASTE

SPICY OLIVE OIL

(continued) ▶

Squeeze all of the juice from the orange cores. You should have about ¼ cup of juice. Pour into a blender along with the reserved orange zest. Add the lemon juice and sea salt. Turn the blender on high and slowly stream in the olive oil. This is your vinaigrette. Set aside in the refrigerator with the orange segments.

To prepare the fennel: Cut the tops from the fennel bulbs and reserve. Peel the tough outer layers and oxidized bottom from each bulb and discard (or reserve for making stock). Cut two of the bulbs into 8 small wedges each.

In a small bowl, combine ¼ cup of olive oil with the kosher salt. Add the fennel wedges and toss to coat. Pour the remaining tablespoon of olive oil into a pan just large enough to fit the fennel wedges in one layer. Heat over a medium-high flame. When the oil just begins to smoke, add the fennel wedges to the pan and turn the heat down to medium. After about 3 minutes, as the fennel begins to caramelize on the bottom, flip it over and cook until the other side is golden brown, another 3 minutes. Turn each piece on its back, sprinkle with the chile, and add a few tablespoons of water. Cover the pan and transfer to the oven until tender, about 20 minutes. Remove from the pan and squeeze some lemon juice over the top. Set aside and let cool.

Meanwhile, quarter the other two fennel bulbs and, with a mandolin, shave lengthwise into paper-thin slices. Place into a bath of ice water to help stiffen your fennel slices and give them a bit of a curl. Pick the delicate fronds from the fennel tops and place in a separate bowl of ice water so they, too, can perk up.

To finish the salad: Remove the fennel slices and fronds from the ice water and dry well. With a spoon, smear a bit of goat cheese in the middle of each plate.

In a bowl, combine the orange segments, greens, sliced fennel, and roasted fennel and season to taste with a bit of sea salt and a squeeze of lemon juice. Moving quickly, so as not to wilt your salad, add some vinaigrette and mix well. Gently remove each portion of salad from the bowl and lay atop the goat cheese. Place a few more dollops of goat cheese on each salad and sprinkle the crushed hazelnuts on top. Finish each salad with a few beautiful fennel fronds and a drizzle of nice, spicy, extra virgin olive oil.

SERVES 4

CAULIFLOWER SOUP WITH SMOKED TROUT

by **TIM MEYERS, MAS (FARMHOUSE)**

Galen Zamarra's West Village restaurant, Mas, takes its name from the French word for "farmhouse," and his rarified menu is inspired daily by his morning shopping trips to Union Square. This cauliflower soup is surprisingly easy to make at home; the additions of almonds and smoked trout take it from simple to sublime. Save the small cauliflower "crumbs" that are left on the cutting board to use as a crowning garnish.

In a medium saucepan over medium-high heat, warm the oil, then add the apples, leek, and shallot and cook until translucent but not brown, about 6 minutes. Add the thinly sliced cauliflower and cook until it softens and begins to release its moisture, about 10 minutes. Add the sherry, cook for 1 minute, then add the stock. If the stock does not cover the vegetables, add additional water to cover. In a small piece of cheesecloth or muslin, tie up the bay leaf, garlic, and peppercorns, and add to the pot. Bring to just under a boil and simmer for 30 minutes.

Remove the satchel of aromatics and transfer the soup and broth to a blender with the butter. Puree until very smooth, 2 to 3 minutes. (If necessary, puree in two batches). Season with kosher salt and lemon juice. Return to the pot and keep warm.

Preheat the oven to 350°F.

Leaving the skin attached, run your finger along the flesh side of the smoked trout fillet to make sure there are no stray pin bones. Place the fillet skin-side down on a small baking dish and warm for 3 minutes in the oven. Remove the fish from the oven and peel off the skin. Gently flake the fish.

Pour about 10 ounces of soup into each bowl and garnish with cauliflower crumbs, baby greens, olive oil, almonds, and warm smoked trout.

SERVES 4

For the Soup

2 TABLESPOONS VEGETABLE OIL

2 PEELED AND DICED GRANNY SMITH APPLES

1 THINLY SLICED LEEK, WHITE PART ONLY

1 DICED SHALLOT

1 HEAD CAULIFLOWER, ABOUT 2 POUNDS, FLORETS THINLY SLICED, SMALL CRUMBLES RESERVED

2 TABLESPOONS DRY SHERRY

1 QUART VEGETABLE STOCK

1 BAY LEAF

2 SMASHED GARLIC CLOVES

5 WHITE PEPPERCORNS

2 TABLESPOONS UNSALTED BUTTER, DICED SMALL

KOSHER SALT

2 TABLESPOONS LEMON JUICE, FROM 1 LEMON

Garnish

1 4-OUNCE FILLET SMOKED TROUT

¼ CUP ROUGHLY CHOPPED MARCONA ALMONDS

¼ CUP BABY GREENS

ROASTED KABOCHA TOAST WITH FRESH RICOTTA

by **DAN KLUGER, ABC KITCHEN**

You could use any winter squash for this recipe, but kabocha—a Japanese variety with knobby skin that may be orange, grey, or green—has a distinctive nutty flavor chefs love. Peeling and slicing the squash takes more time than simply popping halves into the oven, but your prep work is rewarded: The thin pieces cook quickly, complete with caramelized edges.

Meanwhile on the stovetop, vinegar and maple syrup render the onions both zingy and jammy. Heaped atop easy crostini, each element comes together, balanced by fresh ricotta and pretty strips of late-season mint. Serve it alongside a simple soup or pass it at a Thanksgiving feast.

Preheat the oven to 475°F.

Peel, seed, and quarter the squash and slice thin, about ⅛-inch thick. Transfer to a foil-lined baking sheet and toss with 2 tablespoons of olive oil, salt, and the chili flakes. Spread in one layer and roast, stirring occasionally, for 10 to 12 minutes, or until tender and lightly caramelized.

Heat a large sauté pan over medium heat. Add 1 tablespoon of olive oil and the onions, and season with salt. Cook over high heat for 2 to 3 minutes. Lower the heat to medium and cook until deep golden brown, stirring occasionally, about 15 minutes. Add the vinegar and maple syrup and reduce until syrupy and coating the onions, about 15 more minutes. In a mixing bowl, combine with the roasted squash.

Preheat the broiler on high and adjust the rack to about 4 inches from the heating element. Drizzle the bread with 2 tablespoons of olive oil, getting some on each side. Place on a sheet tray and broil for about 1 to 2 minutes per side, until toasted and golden. Spread 2 to 3 tablespoons of ricotta over the toasts, and then top with about ⅓ cup of the kabocha mix. Top with torn mint and a sprinkle of sea salt.

SERVES 6

Ingredients

1 MEDIUM KABOCHA SQUASH, ABOUT 1½ TO 2 POUNDS

5 TABLESPOONS EXTRA VIRGIN OLIVE OIL, DIVIDED

KOSHER SALT

½ TEASPOON CHILI FLAKES

2 MEDIUM SPANISH ONIONS, QUARTERED AND SLICED ¼-INCH THICK

½ CUP APPLE CIDER VINEGAR

¼ CUP MAPLE SYRUP

6 SLICES RUSTIC COUNTRY SOURDOUGH BREAD, SLICED 1-INCH THICK

1 CUP FRESH RICOTTA

4 SPRIGS MINT LEAVES

PINCH COARSE SEA SALT

◀ Hailed as Best New Chef by the James Beard Foundation and *Food & Wine* magazine, Kluger takes literal "field trips" to the farms that fuel his menus. (Amanda Gentile)

Farmers ZAID AND HAIFA KURDIEH

NORWICH MEADOWS FARM

In a world of deceptive advertising and faux-farmy packaging, many market shoppers are there to meet the farmer and get the straight story on exactly how each ingredient was grown.

For both ecological practices and honest answers, they can do no better than Zaid and Haifa Kurdieh. Sure, their farm, Norwich Meadows, is certified organic, but far beyond that word, they'll tell you exactly how each plant and animal lived and died. Such integrity is essential to their farm in part because of their Islamic faith.

"It's very important that Haifa and I are here, personally answering questions completely forthrightly," explains Zaid. "If we had a staffer who said, for example, that our chickens never eat corn, we would have to answer for that. Because on the day of judgment, if you took a single penny in a way that didn't involve full honesty, you can go to hell for it."

Born in Los Angeles to a Palestinian father and American mother, Zaid split his childhood between California and the Middle East. After college, he worked as an agricultural economist, first for the USDA in South Dakota and then at Cornell University. In 1998 he started his own little vegetable "farm"—just half an acre behind the house—but in 2000 his business partner bought 80 acres, and Norwich Meadows has been growing ever since. Today they farm every inch of that land, plus another 29 acres up the road, and an additional 25 acres in New

Jersey. Zaid and his family work tirelessly, and the results speak for themselves.

"I grow a tomato, and so do two hundred other farmers," said Zaid, explaining what drives his decisions. "So why should people buy mine? Between varietals, soil differences, irrigation, and how we treat the plants, we do everything we can to influence the flavor of our product as best we can."

In their cold Central New York climate, intensive agriculture and smart intercropping help them maximize resources and extend the season. By the time the peas are picked, for example, the beans planted between them are already a foot tall.

Such practices allow them to grow enough food for a half-dozen busy markets a week, from Tompkins Square Park to Tucker Square, their stand overflowing with abundant bumper crops: fava beans, fragrant melons, eggplants of all colors, riotous tomatoes, biodiverse beans, purple okra, pink gingerroot, winter squashes from kabocha to sweet dumpling, and a dozen different varieties of Persian cucumbers. "We pick everything in many different sizes," Zaid explains, "from teeny tiny baby stuff chefs want to much larger and cheaper. We're trying to hit everybody's budget."

His expansions also include honey, eggs, halal chicken, and now halal turkey—the poultry slaughtered in a gleaming processing facility right on his own farm. They're even busy in a rented kitchen roasting tomato sauce, simmering up husk-cherry jam, and pickling ginger.

"We want to have everything under the sun, all organic—the widest possible variety of food that tastes really fantastic."

◀ *Zaid worked as an agricultural economist before founding his own organic farm, which grows everything from Persian cucumbers to gingerroot. "We want to have everything under the sun," he says.* (Amanda Gentile)

(continued) ▶

That pursuit drove him to put down roots in warmer New Jersey. Crops like okra, for example, were limited in Chenango County, where summer starts late and ends early. Down in Jersey, the happy plants grow 10 feet tall.

His produce is gorgeous, but for him, appearances are immaterial. "We're always accused, 'How can you be organic, these things look too good.' But perfect-looking produce is really not the point for me. Instead, when they taste it, I want them to say, 'Wow, this is different.'"

Perfect-looking produce is really not the point for me. Instead, when they taste it, I want them to say, "Wow, this is different."

Despite the farm's busy expansion, it would have grown even more quickly were it not for the Kurdiehs' faith. Islam prohibits monetary interest, both taking and giving, so the business is 100 percent reliant on cash flow. "We could probably grow even more and do even better things," explains Zaid, "but I can't just go to the bank and get a half-million dollar loan. Luckily John Deere has a zero percent financing program, but large ticket items—a piece of land or even a truck—has to come out of our cash flow or retirement."

But Islam's main guiding principle, explains Zaid, is peace. Which includes caring for the land and the animals in his charge. "We, and the people we hire," says Zaid, "treat our birds like living things until the very last minute."

While chefs may admire Zaid's integrity, it's fair to wager most love him for his food's flavor. In the past few years, restaurant orders have grown to nearly half his sales. At Union Square, they have a separate tent dedicated just to chef customers, who come from Danny Meyer's kitchens, plus Craft, Craft Bar, 'wich Craft, Blue Hill, Il Buco, Boulud, the Marlow group, and many more. They follow their noses here—or rather, their mouths.

"Dan Barber was at the stand," says Zaid. "He said, 'I want something *really* fantastic.' I told him, 'Taste this pepper. It's called Lunchbox pepper. It's long and narrow, very sweet, very tasty.' He loved it. He bought it all."

But arguably their closest relationship is with Chef Mike Anthony of Gramercy Tavern, who cooked Norwich produce for his family for a year before he started buying for the restaurant, too.

Gramercy Tavern is just a few blocks north of Union Square, and the geographic and emotional proximity has led to a twice-weekly tradition: lunch.

Zaid and Haifa leave the stand for an hour and stroll up Broadway to eat in the restaurant's casual front room in their market T-shirts and aprons, recognizing their own crops on the plate. "It's a business relationship," says Zaid, "but it's also a family relationship."

They've worked hard to get where they are—and they're planning even more. "It's staggering growth," says Zaid. "We can't believe where we're at. Now I'm hoping to add 30 acres of land that adjoin my house. We're up to 6 acres of high tunnels. And, God willing, we'll do another 5 acres next year."

SPICY SWEET POTATO SALAD

by **TAMAR ADLER, AUTHOR OF** *AN EVERLASTING MEAL*

Forget the brown sugar and marshmallows—topping baked sweet potatoes with lime, jalapeño, cilantro, and mint takes them to Vietnam. The shower of green makes the dish gorgeously fresh, and while it packs some heat, the herbs and lime are so refreshing that you'll want to make this in summer too. Just pop your sweet potatoes in the oven anytime it's on; once baked, they'll keep for several days in the fridge until you're ready to make this bright, surprising salad.

Preheat the oven to 400°F.

Prick the sweet potatoes with a fork and bake on a foil-lined baking sheet for about an hour, until the skins are wrinkled and the flesh is completely tender.

Let the potatoes cool on the counter, then place them in the refrigerator to firm up. Meanwhile, combine the jalapeño and shallot in a large bowl with a pinch of salt and the lime juice. Allow to sit for at least 10 minutes or up to a few hours.

When the sweet potatoes are cold, peel and cut them into thick rounds, then add the macerated shallots and jalapeño, plus the olive oil, the herbs, and the salt. Toss gently to combine. Garnish with chopped peanuts and serve.

SERVES 4

2½ POUNDS LARGE SWEET POTATOES, ABOUT 2 TO 3

1 FINELY CHOPPED JALAPEÑO, SEEDS INCLUDED

1 LARGE, THINLY SLICED SHALLOT OR ¼ RED ONION

3 TABLESPOONS FRESH LIME JUICE, FROM ABOUT 3 WHOLE LIMES

2 TABLESPOONS EXTRA VIRGIN OLIVE OIL

¼ CUP ROUGHLY CHOPPED MINT

¼ CUP ROUGHLY CHOPPED CILANTRO

¼ CUP CHOPPED, ROASTED PEANUTS

SALT

KOHLRABI SLAW

by **LIZ NEUMARK, GREAT PERFORMANCES AND KATCHKIE FARM**

2 TABLESPOONS CIDER VINEGAR

3 TABLESPOONS LEMON JUICE, FROM ABOUT 1 LEMON

¼ CUP MAYONNAISE

¼ CUP YOGURT

½ THINLY SLICED GREEN ONION, ABOUT ¼ CUP

1 TEASPOON SALT

½ TEASPOON BLACK PEPPER

2 TABLESPOONS CHOPPED PARSLEY

2 TABLESPOONS CHOPPED CHIVES

2 TABLESPOONS CHOPPED MINT

3 TO 4 MEDIUM PEELED KOHLRABIS

2 PEELED CARROTS

Kohlrabi probably ties with celeriac as the vegetable that draws the strangest looks at market. But this deliciously versatile ingredient is well worth getting to know.

Cut open a kohlrabi and inside you'll find crisp, white flesh that looks like apple but tastes like cabbage. "Kohl," after all, is German for cabbage, and kohlrabi is a close cousin of cauliflower, kale, and the rest of the family that farmers call "cole crops." This lesser-known Brassica can be eaten cooked or raw; here it stands in for cabbage in a quick slaw that's both juicy and crunchy. The yogurt, herbs, and lemon make it bright and fresh alongside any meat or fish.

In a large mixing bowl, combine the cider vinegar, lemon juice, mayonnaise, yogurt, green onion, salt, pepper, parsley, chives, and mint. Whisk to combine.

In the large bowl of a food processor or with a box grater, grate the kohlrabi and carrot. Add to the mixing bowl with the dressing and toss well to combine. Season with additional salt and pepper to taste. Chill for a few hours and toss again before serving.

SERVES 6

FRISÉE AND FENNEL WITH CHEDDAR AND ROASTED PEARS

by **MARCO MOREIRA, TOCQUEVILLE**

This frisée-pear-balsamic combination is such a classic, Tocqueville has featured the salad on its menu for nearly a decade. When you make it with superior, in-season ingredients, you can see why customers still crave it.

Be sure to begin with ripe pears. Roasted, they'll become soft and sweet; a final minute under the broiler gives them caramelized edges. You could serve them for dessert, but instead they're balanced by the bitterness of fresh frisée and the crunch of raw fennel.

The Bloomsday cheddar is what makes the dish. Cato Corner Farm crafts this raw cow's-milk cheese each year on the holiday honoring James Joyce, on June 16. It's available at different ages; at just six months old, the bite is medium-sharp, but the eighteen-month aged Bloomsday is creamy, sharp, and wonderfully nutty with a lingering aftertaste.

Preheat the oven to 425°F.

Cut each pear into quarters or sixths, depending on the size, and remove the cores. Place in a large mixing bowl and drizzle with the maple syrup and melted butter, season with salt and black pepper, and toss to combine. Arrange on a sheet tray and roast for 15 to 20 minutes, tossing halfway through. Finish under the broiler for 1 minute to caramelize the edges. Remove and let cool.

Place the sherry vinegar in a medium bowl and add the olive oil in a thin stream, whisking quickly to emulsify. Season with salt and pepper to taste.

In a medium bowl, mix the frisée with the fennel, toss with the vinaigrette, and season with salt and pepper to taste. Place 2 to 3 pieces of pear on each plate and top with the dressed salad, a slice of cheddar, and a handful of toasted nuts.

SERVES 6 TO 8

4 SMALL BOSC PEARS

¼ CUP MAPLE SYRUP

2 TABLESPOONS MELTED, UNSALTED BUTTER

3 TABLESPOONS SHERRY VINEGAR

6 TABLESPOONS OLIVE OIL

SALT AND PEPPER

1 HEAD WASHED AND DRIED FRISÉE, CORE DISCARDED

1 FENNEL BULB, SLICED PAPER THIN

8 OUNCES FARMSTEAD CHEDDAR, SUCH AS CATO CORNER'S BLOOMSDAY

1 CUP TOASTED AND ROUGHLY CHOPPED HAZELNUTS OR WALNUTS

PAN-SEARED SCALLOPS WITH APPLE CIDER BROWN BUTTER AND BRUSSELS SPROUTS-APPLE SLAW

by **CARMEN QUAGLIATA, UNION SQUARE CAFÉ**

Slaw

1 SMALL- TO MEDIUM-SIZED CORED HONEYCRISP APPLE

7 LARGE BRUSSELS SPROUTS

1 TABLESPOON FRESH SQUEEZED LEMON JUICE, FROM ABOUT ½ LEMON

1 TEASPOON APPLE CIDER VINEGAR

SALT AND FRESHLY GROUND BLACK PEPPER

2 TABLESPOONS EXTRA VIRGIN OLIVE OIL

Scallops

16 LARGE SCALLOPS, ABDUCTOR MUSCLES REMOVED

SALT AND BLACK PEPPER

2 TABLESPOONS VEGETABLE OIL

5 TABLESPOONS UNSALTED BUTTER

6 TORN SAGE LEAVES

1 TABLESPOON FRESH SQUEEZED LEMON JUICE, FROM ABOUT ½ LEMON

6 TABLESPOONS APPLE CIDER

Danny Meyer founded his hospitality empire with Union Square Café just a stone's throw from the Greenmarket back in 1985 and has since been famous for his farm-centric fare—like this light dish, which cooks in less than fifteen minutes. Scallops are simply seared—just a minute or two per side—then their pan juices become an autumnal sauce with apple cider and nutty browned butter that will make you want to lick your plate clean. A quick Brussels sprouts slaw is also a snap to prepare and features the Honeycrisp apple, whose extraordinary crunchiness inspires a cult following each fall. To make this appetizer into a main, serve over creamy polenta.

Prepare the slaw: Using a mandolin or a sharp knife, shave or finely slice the apple into short matchsticks. Shave or thinly slice the Brussels sprouts and toss with the apples in a bowl. Dress with the lemon juice, apple cider vinegar, salt, pepper, and olive oil, and toss to coat. Set aside.

Prepare the scallops: Pat the scallops very dry with a paper towel. Season both sides of each scallop with salt and pepper. Heat the vegetable oil in a 10-inch sauté pan over medium-high heat until wavy but not smoking. Remove the pan from the heat to add the scallops, then return to medium-low heat. Cook until the scallops are nicely browned on one side, 1 to 2 minutes. Turn the scallops over and cook the other side for another minute—they might not be as brown as the first side, but that's okay. Transfer to a plate, dark side up.

Pour out the oil or blot the pan with a paper towel. Add the butter and return the pan to medium heat. When the butter is bubbly and golden brown, remove from heat and add the sage leaves to sizzle. Then add the lemon juice, apple cider, and a pinch of salt. Swirl all ingredients together and return the pan to the heat, bringing to a full boil while scraping the browned bits off the bottom. Once the liquid boils, reduce heat to low and add the scallops, dark side up, and any juices that may have gathered on their plate. Lightly simmer until the sauce is smooth and thickened, swirling occasionally to keep combined, about 1 minute.

Place the scallops on individual plates with a couple of spoonfuls of apple cider-brown butter over each. Add a bundle of the slaw to each and serve.

SERVES 4

Farmer ELIZABETH GILLMAN
CATO CORNER FARM

"It became apparent that making cheese would be a very good idea."

So recalls Elizabeth Gillman of a realization she arrived at twenty years ago. She had been raising goats on her Connecticut farm since 1979, but each time she sold the young animals for meat, her herd of nannies suddenly had an abundance of milk. And you know what they say about when life gives you lemons.

Elizabeth had loved cheese since childhood and after some experiments taught herself to make her surplus goat milk into sophisticated chèvre. Before long she added Jersey cows, which are prized for their milk's high butterfat content.

After a cheese chemistry intensive and a hands-on class with a Belgian cheesemaker, she set to handling curd and washing rinds; by 1997 her first aged, raw-milk cows cheeses were ready for their debut at the Greenmarket. It's hard to believe that back then, only three participants sold cheese, including an Amish farm that sold vacuum-packed blocks alongside their shoo-fly pie. The phrase "American cheese" still conjured images of fluorescent orange, plastic-wrapped slices, and most people thought serious cheese was something you imported from Europe.

At home in what Gillman calls "conservative Connecticut," appetites were limited to brie, but at city Greenmarkets—on the Upper West Side, near the United Nations, down in Tribeca, and over in Park Slope—she found a warm reception, as samplers quickly became shoppers.

◄ *Initially, Elizabeth was like the little red hen—milking cows, making cheese, and selling it herself. Now seventy, she still tends the herd and milks them at four o'clock each morning.* (Amanda Gentile)

Initially, Elizabeth was like the little red hen—milking a dozen cows, making their milk into cheese, and selling it all in the city herself. But help arrived in the form of her son, Mark, who quit his job as an English teacher to move back to the family farm. Soon selections ran the gamut from the mild, nutty Brigid's Abbey to the stinky, gooey washed-rind Hooligan, all proudly "farmstead," meaning they contain only milk from the farm's own herd. That grass-fed milk's high beta-carotene content turns the curd a signature golden hue.

Selections ran the gamut from the mild, nutty Brigid's Abbey to the stinky, gooey washed-rind Hooligan, all proudly "farmstead," meaning they contain only milk from the farm's own herd.

While Mark turns out wittily named offerings like Womanchego, Dairyere, Misty Morning, and Vivace, his mother, now seventy, still tends the herd and milks her forty-two cows at four o'clock each morning. Not only does the family not buy milk from other farms—they also do not buy cows. Every single animal in the herd—with names such as Dana, Shiobhan, and Dierdre—was born on the farm. And unlike most dairies, they never ship their bull calves to auction, instead raising them for beef or veal, which they sell at the farm.

A 2001 grant helped finance an underground cave with precise conditions for aging and storing. Elizabeth laughs that it's not some gleaming state-of-the art facility, but the temperature and humidity boosted both their quality and quantity, helping them land awards from the esteemed American Cheese Society and praise from magazines such as *Saveur* and pride of place on the menu at many top Manhattan restaurants.

But for Elizabeth, all those successes are inconsequential compared to protecting her farm; she once declined an $800,000 offer for the land that would have had her pastures bulldozed into housing tracts. Her decades-long preservation dream came true when she arranged not one but two conservation easements on the property: A federal program now protects her farm fields in perpetuity, while the Connecticut Farmland Trust preserves the woods, wetlands, and ledges. Today the whole property is permanently protected from commercial development.

It's the payoff for Elizabeth's decades of dedication, but she says it never would have been possible without her city sales. "It all worked because of Greenmarket," she says. "If we hadn't been able to go to New York, we wouldn't have been able to make it. No way. No way."

FLAT IRON STEAK WITH FREEKEH AND PEPPERS

by **MICHAEL ANTHONY, EXECUTIVE CHEF AT GRAMERCY TAVERN**

This recipe calls for four components, but each is simple enough that you can make the whole delicious dish in less than one hour. The surprise here is that the peppers are cooked two ways—half are roasted and half are sautéed. You could, of course, prepare them all one way or the other, but the combination is beautiful, with the roasted peppers silky and sweet while the sautéed peppers retain their fresh texture. The freekeh is hearty while the Flat Iron steak cooks quickly and delivers a strong, meaty flavor.

Heat a 4-quart saucepan over medium heat until warm. Add 1 tablespoon of olive oil, the diced onion, and a pinch of salt. Sweat for about 5 minutes, stirring occasionally, until soft and translucent. Add the freekeh and stir to combine. Toast the freekeh for about 2 minutes. Begin to add 2 cups of water, ½ cup at a time as the freekeh cooks, and let simmer until the grains are tender but still have a bite, 35 to 40 minutes. Cover and set aside.

Preheat the oven to 350°F.

Slice the peppers and red onion into strips, about ½-inch wide. Toss half of the peppers and onions with 1 tablespoon of olive oil and a pinch of salt and pepper. Transfer to a foil-lined sheet pan and roast until tender, about 30 minutes.

Meanwhile, heat a 10-inch sauté pan over medium heat. Add 1 tablespoon of olive oil, then the remaining peppers and onions. Season with salt and cook until tender, for 5 to 6 minutes.

Combine all peppers and onions with the freekeh. Set aside.

3 TABLESPOONS OLIVE OIL, DIVIDED

½ CUP DICED YELLOW ONION, ABOUT ½ MEDIUM ONION

1 CUP FREEKEH

2 BELL PEPPERS

1 ANCHO PEPPER

1 CUBANELLE PEPPER

1 MEDIUM RED ONION

1½ POUNDS FLAT IRON STEAK, AT ROOM TEMPERATURE

1 TABLESPOON VEGETABLE OIL

¼ CUP ROUGHLY CHOPPED BASIL LEAVES

¼ CUP ROUGHLY CHOPPED PARSLEY LEAVES

2 TEASPOONS SHERRY VINEGAR

SALT AND FRESHLY GROUND BLACK PEPPER TO TASTE

(continued) ▶

Pat the beef dry and season each side with salt and pepper. Heat a 12-inch sauté pan over medium-high heat. Add the vegetable oil and heat until it shimmers, then add the beef. Cook to desired doneness for 3 minutes per side or until the center reaches 120°F. Remove from the pan and let rest for 5 to 10 minutes before slicing.

While the beef is resting, add 1 tablespoon of water to the freekeh-pepper mixture and warm it over medium-low heat, stirring occasionally until warmed through, about 4 to 5 minutes. Add the basil, parsley, sherry vinegar, and salt and pepper to taste. Divide evenly among four plates and top with sliced Flat Iron steak.

SERVES 4

◀ Chef Anthony is one of the most respected chefs in the country, but he likes to pass the credit along to the farmers he's been buying from for years. (Amanda Gentile)

SLOW-COOKED TURKEY IN GREEN MOLE

by **JACQUES GAUTIER, PALO SANTO**

It's an open secret that when it comes to turkey, most people prefer the sides. But that's because the supermarket birds on many Thanksgiving tables are pathetically short on flavor, thanks to a lifetime eating grain indoors and breeding for breast meat, not taste. Once you've tasted a pastured turkey, especially the dark meat of a traditional heritage breed such as a Bourbon Red, you won't want to wait until Thanksgiving for your next plate.

Our national bird is native to America, and in this dish Chef Jacques gives it the Latino treatment with tomatillo, chile pepper, cilantro, and beer—for the latter, we recommend Greenmarket Wheat, fermented by Brooklyn Brewery using upstate grain, as well as wildflower honey, and Massachusetts malt. When finishing this recipe, don't skip the reduction step at the end—simmering the sauce for a final fifteen minutes makes it deliciously thick.

1 POUND GREEN TOMATILLOS, HUSKS REMOVED

1 TABLESPOON OLIVE OIL

3 POUNDS TURKEY PARTS (DRUMSTICKS, BREAST, AND/OR THIGHS)

1 LARGE, THINLY SLICED YELLOW ONION

6 ROUGHLY CHOPPED GARLIC CLOVES

1 CHOPPED SERRANO CHILE

1 12-OUNCE CAN LIGHT BEER

2 CUPS CHICKEN OR LIGHT TURKEY STOCK

1 BUNCH CILANTRO, LEAVES AND STEMS SEPARATED, STEMS TIED INTO A BUNDLE WITH KITCHEN TWINE

2 LIMES, JUICED, ABOUT ¼ CUP

SALT AND FRESHLY GROUND BLACK PEPPER

Preheat the oven to 300°F.

Puree the tomatillos in a blender until smooth.

Heat the olive oil in a large Dutch oven over medium high heat. Season all sides of the turkey pieces with salt and pepper and sear 2 to 3 pieces at a time, until golden brown on all sides. Place the seared turkey on a plate and reserve the fat in the pot.

Reduce heat to medium and add the onion, garlic, and chile to the pot and cook until golden brown, 7 to 8 minutes. Deglaze with the beer and bring to a simmer, then add the tomatillo puree and chicken stock, return to a simmer and add the turkey and the bunched cilantro stems. Cover and transfer to the center rack of the oven. Cook until the meat is tender and falling off the bone, about 2 hours.

(continued) ▶

Remove the turkey from the sauce and rest until cool enough to handle. Remove the cilantro stems and discard. Place the Dutch oven on the stovetop over medium heat. Simmer uncovered and reduce the liquid by half, until thickened, about 20 minutes. Remove from the heat and stir in the cilantro leaves and lime juice. Adjust seasoning with salt and pepper.

Meanwhile, once the turkey is cool enough to handle, discard the skin, remove the meat from the bone, and shred. Transfer the turkey to a large serving bowl and cover with enough sauce to moisten the meat. Serve alongside a starchy side such as corn tortillas or rice and beans.

SERVES 6 TO 8

Farmer FRED WILKLOW
WILKLOW ORCHARDS

Fred Wilklow's great-great-grandfather established the family orchard in the hills of a town called Pancake Hollow back in 1855; a century later, when Fred was growing up, the farm grew exactly one thing—apples— which the Wilklows sold wholesale to area grocery stores.

But by the time Fred was twenty-seven, food was being trucked long distances and the USDA mantra was "get big or get out." As prices fell in a race to the bottom, the wholesale market wasn't covering the Wilklows' costs, much less yielding a profit. Fred was the fifth generation to farm this land, married with two young children, and losing money on every case of apples he sold.

Orchards all around him were unable to sell their fruit for a fair price, but Fred found a way: the Greenmarket. He applied in 1984 and landed a spot at Brooklyn Borough Hall starting that June. It was about twenty years before Brooklyn became the American capital of the locavore revolution, but even back then Brooklynites knew good apples when they saw them. Which meant Fred could keep farming.

"Growing fruit well isn't enough," he said recently. "You have to be able to sell it, too. If you can't turn your crop back into money, you don't have anything."

His new city customers didn't just turn his apples back into money—he saw that they had an appetite for other fruits, too, which led him back to the farm's more diverse roots. He planted peaches, plums, nectarines, pears, cherries, blueberries, even gooseberries. (Fred later discovered records from 1919 that showed the farm had boasted seven thousand currant

◀ *"Growing fruit well isn't enough," says Fred. "You have to be able to sell it, too."*

bushes back then; he grows them, too, mostly red. His favorite way to eat them is in pancakes, where their tartness is a welcome contrast.)

Fred's Greenmarket sales not only financed more trees—he was able to invest in infrastructure, too, eventually building a bakery, controlled-atmosphere storage, and greenhouses, growing not just food for his customers, but a business for his family. He bought more land. He even started raising pigs and cows. But most of all, he planted more apple trees, including many varieties, both old and new.

Ulster County's hills are too rocky to plow but ideal for orchards.

It was about twenty years before Brooklyn became the American capital of the locavore revolution, but even back then Brooklynites knew good apples when they saw them. Which meant Fred could keep farming.

"We specialize in what we do best," Fred says. The land may be too rocky and sloped to easily plow, but the Ulster County hills are widely renowned for their microclimate, ideal for growing tree fruit.

From tart greenings in late July to the Winesaps, Fujis, and Honeycrisps they pick into November, the Wilklows bring dozens of diverse varieties of apples to the Big Apple. They also welcome New Yorkers to their farm—every October, thousands of people visit Wilklow Orchards for pick-your-own apples, complete with hayrides and hot cider donuts.

And like Fred, who had a young family when he first gave Greenmarket a shot, his children now have young kids of their own and are hitching their future to selling in the city.

Thirty years after their first day at market, Fred has expanded the farm from 40 acres to more than 200, all within 5 miles of the original home farm. Today his four children, all grown, are employed on the farm—tending the trees, making preserves and pies, handling paperwork, even fermenting hard cider. In other words, they've come a long way.

"We were a small, mostly apple farm, struggling in the wholesale market. We found Greenmarket and are now extremely diversified," says Fred, looking back. "Now we grow every kind of fruit, and our farm expanded as our family grew. Greenmarket has done that. It made us a successful farm that's able to sustain our family. We now have five families living off this farm. And my grandkids are the seventh generation."

SAUTÉED FLUKE WITH ROASTED JERUSALEM ARTICHOKES, TOASTED PUMPKIN SEEDS, AND PICKLED CELERY

by **KATHERINE YOUNGBLOOD, LOT 2**

Pickled Celery

½ CUP WHITE WINE VINEGAR

¼ CUP GRANULATED SUGAR

2 TABLESPOONS SALT

4 RIBS CELERY, SLICED CROSSWISE ¼-INCH

Fluke

1 POUND JERUSALEM ARTICHOKES, SCRUBBED WELL

SALT

2 TABLESPOONS OLIVE OIL

¼ TEASPOON CHILI FLAKES

2 MINCED GARLIC CLOVES

4 5-OUNCE FLUKE FILLETS, SKIN REMOVED

2 TABLESPOONS GRAPESEED OR VEGETABLE OIL, DIVIDED

1 LEMON, QUARTERED

¼ CUP TOASTED PUMPKIN SEEDS (SEE HEADNOTE)

¼ CUP YELLOW CELERY LEAVES FROM A BUNCH'S INNER RIBS

Jerusalem artichokes look like knobby potatoes crossed with ginger root, but they have a wonderfully sweet, nutty flavor like nothing you've ever tasted. The tubers grow amid the roots of certain varieties of towering sunflowers, which gives them their other name: sunchokes. Roasted, they develop a silky-soft center and crispy skin that, in this dish, plays off the flaky fluke and the crunch of the pumpkin seeds and quick-pickled celery.

Make the pickled celery: Prepare the brine by bringing the vinegar, sugar, salt, and ¼ cup plus 2 tablespoons of water to a boil in a saucepan. Meanwhile, place the prepared celery in a medium bowl. Once the brine comes to a boil, give it a stir to make sure the sugar has dissolved, and then pour over the sliced celery. Let the celery pickle for at least 1 hour before using. (You can prepare the pickled celery up to a week ahead; refrigerate once cooled.)

Prepare the fluke: Preheat the oven to 400°F.

If the Jerusalem artichokes are smaller than 1 inch, then leave them whole (some are the size of marbles). Otherwise, cut into 1-inch pieces. In a bowl, toss them with 1 teaspoon of salt and the olive oil. Place on a sheet tray or roasting pan and roast for 35 minutes or until golden and tender, stirring after 15 minutes and rotating the pan for even roasting. Once roasted, reserve them on the sheet pan, and turn the oven down to 350°F.

To the tray of Jerusalem artichokes, add the chili flakes and garlic. Strain the celery, discard the brine, and add the celery to the tray and toss to combine. While the fish cooks, reheat the tray in the oven for 7 to 8 minutes.

(continued) ▶

Season the fluke on both sides with salt. Heat 1 tablespoon of grapeseed oil in a large sauté pan, cast-iron pan, or nonstick skillet over high heat. When the oil shimmers, add 2 fillets and cook for about 2 minutes or until golden. Flip and cook for another minute. Squeeze ¼ of the lemon all over the fish, remove from the pan and keep warm. Repeat with remaining tablespoon of oil and 2 fillets.

Squeeze the remaining two quarters of the lemon on the warm Jerusalem artichoke mixture and toss to combine. Serve the fluke on top of the Jerusalem artichokes and celery, garnished with toasted pumpkin seeds and yellow celery leaves.

SERVES 4

Here is another kind of seed saver:

When Americans cook winter squash, such as pumpkin or butternut, we typically toss out the seeds and cook only the sweet orange flesh—but Austrians do just the opposite! Next time you've got a pile of slimy seeds, simply spread them on a sheet pan, season with a little oil and salt (or not), and bake at 350°F for 30 to 45 minutes, until they're as crunchy as you like. They make great, protein-rich snacks, can be tossed in any salad, or, in this case, add a wonderfully crunchy garnish to a simple fish dish. If you like, season with anything from cayenne to cinnamon.

PASTA WITH BRUSSELS SPROUTS AND BACON

by **SARA JENKINS, PORSENA AND PORCHETTA**

Leave it to Sara Jenkins to create a pasta that's simple enough to throw together on a weeknight but delicious enough that your company will beg for the recipe. It can be tempting to shred these sprouts, but separate them instead and you'll see why Jenkins says, "What makes this pasta for me is the integrity of the individual leaves." Peeling each leaf off the top is slow going—instead the trick is to work *from the bottom*, lopping off not just the stem, but the bottom quarter of each sprout. Then you can quickly peel from the stem end, trimming the base as you go to release more leaves. (If you mince the hearts, we won't tell Chef Jenkins.)

With the unctuous bacon balanced by the brightness of thyme, even a Brussels sprouts skeptic will want thirds. This is a dish you'll find yourself making weekly, well into winter.

1 POUND BRUSSELS SPROUTS

2 TABLESPOONS UNSALTED BUTTER

2 TABLESPOONS EXTRA VIRGIN OLIVE OIL

3 OUNCES THICK-CUT BACON OR PANCETTA (ABOUT 2 STRIPS), CUT CROSSWISE INTO ½-INCH STRIPS

1 TABLESPOON FRESH THYME LEAVES

1 POUND ARTISAN-DRIED SHORT PASTA SUCH AS PENNETTE OR MACCHERONCINI

SALT AND PEPPER

½ CUP GRATED PARMIGIANO-REGGIANO

Trim the bottom quarter off each Brussels sprout and separate each head into individual leaves (see headnote).

In a large sauté pan, melt the butter with olive oil over medium heat. Add the bacon and render the fat out gently until it starts to crisp, about 8 minutes. Increase the heat and add the Brussels sprouts leaves in handfuls, letting them wilt and crisp a bit in the pan, about 4 to 5 minutes. Add the thyme and a pinch of salt. Set aside.

Bring a large stockpot of water to a boil, season generously with salt, add the pasta, and cook according to the manufacturer's instructions. Reserve ¼ cup of the pasta water. Strain the pasta and keep warm in a large mixing bowl.

Toss the Brussels sprouts and bacon with the pasta in the mixing bowl and add the Parmigiano-Reggiano, fresh cracked pepper, and 2 to 4 tablespoons of pasta water to moisten the pasta, as needed. Adjust the salt and serve.

PASTA WITH SWISS CHARD AND CANNELLINI

by **MARK LADNER, DEL POSTO**

2 BUNCHES SWISS CHARD, ABOUT 1½ POUNDS

3 TABLESPOONS OLIVE OIL

1 FINELY CHOPPED JALAPEÑO

2 THINLY SLICED GARLIC CLOVES

1 LARGE, DICED RED ONION

2 CUPS COOKED CANNELLINI BEANS

1 POUND FRESH LINGUINE OR FETTUCCINE

1 TABLESPOON UNSALTED BUTTER

1 CUP FINELY GRATED PARMIGIANO-REGGIANO CHEESE

2 TABLESPOONS LEMON JUICE, FROM ABOUT 1 LEMON

Two bunches of Swiss chard? Yes, you read that correctly. Beets' leafy "goosefoot" cousin cooks down so much, you may wish you'd put in even more—especially when you're licking the pan of this rustic, hearty ragù.

Use any color chard—red, white, or the neon-stemmed varieties called "bright lights." The leaves cook more quickly than the stalks, but they're easy to separate—just hold each piece by the stem and rip away the tender greens, or lay each leaf on a cutting board, folded lengthwise at the spine, and slice the ribs away.

Fresh shell beans simmer up in a quick twenty minutes, but if you're starting with dried—say from Race Farm or Cayuga Pure Organics—soak 1 cup for 5 hours or overnight, then add a bay leaf and 4 smashed garlic cloves and simmer for an hour or until tender; season with 2 teaspoons of salt and a glug of olive oil. Beans may be cooked 3 to 4 days ahead and refrigerated in their cooking liquid.

Bring a large pot of water to a boil. Season generously with salt so it tastes like the ocean.

Separate the leaves from the stems of the Swiss chard and rinse well. Chop the stems into ½-inch pieces and the leaves into 2-inch pieces.

Heat a large Dutch oven over medium heat, add the olive oil, then the jalapeño and garlic and bloom for 1 minute. Add the onion and reduce heat to medium low. Sweat until tender, about 5 minutes. Add the chard stems and sweat about 3 to 5 minutes until completely tender. Add the chard leaves, ¼ cup of water, and a pinch of salt. Increase the heat to medium high, cover with a lid, and cook for about 2 minutes, then remove the lid and stir well to cook all of the chard leaves evenly.

Add the beans, stir well, and simmer for 5 minutes, allowing the flavors to come together.

Meanwhile, cook the pasta according to package directions until al dente. Reserve 2 tablespoons of pasta water and drain the pasta. To the chard mixture, add the pasta, pasta water, butter, cheese, and lemon juice. Simmer for 1 to 2 more minutes for the flavors to meld and the sauce to coat the pasta.

SERVES 6

Farmer DAN GIBSON
GRAZIN' ANGUS ACRES

Dan Gibson named his Hudson Valley farm after what he raises: Black Angus. It's the same beef breed that fills seemingly endless Texas feedlots and tops endless McDonald's buns. But black hide aside, Grazin' Angus Acres has precisely nothing in common with the so-called farms where his cattle's unlucky cousins live and die.

The difference lies in the rest of the farm's name. These beeves spend their days grazing Gibson's 450 acres of pasture, where the magic of photosynthesis and the food chain transform pure sunshine into 100 percent grass-fed beef that's arguably as ecologically responsible as a head of lettuce.

Up in Columbia County, New York, his peers are people whose families have been farming for generations, but Gibson arrived in agriculture via a very different path. Just a few years ago, he was senior vice president at Starwood Hotels and Resorts, managing chic brands such as W and Le Meridien and calling posh Westchester home. But the events of 9/11 inspired him to pursue a more grounded life, which led to a somewhat unusual purchase: a Hudson Valley dairy farm he had no idea what to do with until a casual conversation changed everything. Chatting with one of his Wall Street clients, Gibson learned the man was father to two autistic children and felt sure that America's food supply was at least in part to blame. Gibson was fascinated with the idea that our industrialized diet could be wreaking widespread havoc on public health and, shortly after, devoured an early copy of Michael

◀ *Gibson managed chic hotel brands like W and Le Meridien until the events of 9/11 inspired him to pursue a more grounded life.*

Pollan's *The Omnivore's Dilemma.* "I got absolutely passionate about it," he said. "It's my bible."

Inspired to raise the kind of meat that's all but a memory in the twenty-first century, Gibson and his wife, Susan, moved to Ghent full-time in 2007. But even though he traded his suit for blue jeans, he hardly put himself out to pasture. He and his family work dawn to dusk, moving cows to fresh grass, setting up electric fencing, and tending pastured pigs and chickens. His animals put on weight much more slowly than those in industrial operations, but their longer lives and "grass and only grass" diet also mean they develop more flavor. Their lives are so good that many of Gibson's Greenmarket customers are longtime vegetarians who say it feels right to eat meat from a farm guided entirely by ecology and animal welfare. Yes, Gibson raises animals for slaughter, but at every step, he does right by them, the land, and the customer.

Through the magic of photosynthesis, pure sunshine becomes 100 percent grass-fed beef.

Many of Gibson's Greenmarket customers are longtime vegetarians who say it feels right to eat meat from a farm guided entirely by ecology and animal welfare.

As if founding a farm wasn't enough to keep him busy, the entrepreneurial-minded Gibson decided to take on even more—twice. Grazin's first expansion came when a stainless-steel art deco diner in the neighboring town of Hudson came up for sale. He quickly rechristened it Grazin' Diner. Today his staff there serves classic fare like burgers and shakes—made with the local, organic ingredients more often found on white tablecloths. Johnny Cash plays on the jukebox, and the walls bear framed photos of the livestock now gracing the plates.

Even the milkshakes are from Gibson's own farm. That's because the 2012 closing of a small dairy farm that was Grazin's neighbor, both upstate and at market, prompted him to add a milking herd to his mix. Today, Gibson and his family tend twenty-four Jersey cows, and like the beef cattle, they're 100 percent grass fed. He sells their rich, organic milk in glass bottles, as well as spinning it into yogurt, butter, and ice cream—with plans to get into cheesemaking, too.

Gibson has since met Pollan, but when the now-farmer shook Pollan's hand, raving, "You changed my life," Gibson realized the writer hears those words every day. "No, you really, really, *really* changed my life," he explained. "I live and breathe this thing!"

FARROTTO WITH FRESH SHELL BEANS, PANCETTA, AND SAGE

by CESARE CASELLA, IL RISTORANTE ROSI AND SALUMERIA ROSI

Fresh Shell Beans

3 CUPS FRESH SHELL BEANS, SUCH AS CRANBERRY OR CANNELLINI, FROM 2 POUNDS OF BEANS IN SHELL

4 GARLIC CLOVES

4 SPRIGS FRESH SAGE

8 PEPPERCORNS

1 TABLESPOON SALT

2 TABLESPOONS OLIVE OIL

Fagioli with Pancetta

¼ CUP EXTRA VIRGIN OLIVE OIL

1 DICED ONION

6 FINELY CHOPPED GARLIC CLOVES

½ CUP CHOPPED PANCETTA (OR BACON)

1 TABLESPOON CHOPPED FRESH SAGE

1 TEASPOON CRUSHED RED PEPPER

3 CUPS FRESH TOMATOES, CRUSHED BY HAND

3 CUPS COOKED CANNELLINI BEANS (FROM ABOVE), COOKING LIQUID RESERVED

SALT AND FRESHLY GROUND BLACK PEPPER

You can use pancetta or bacon in this recipe, but either way, the beans will steal the show. Pork doesn't usually take a back seat to legumes, but Chef Casella knows what he's doing.

Several Greenmarket farmers grow shell beans like cannellini and cranberry to sell dried in winter, and for a few months in fall they're available fresh. Easy to overlook in their papery pods, the mature-but-moist beans need only a simple simmer to take on a velvet texture and true bean flavor you'll never find in a can.

Here they star in a riff on risotto, in which emmer (the wheat berry known in Italy as farro) is slowly stirred with a flavorful broth. It's not the sort of dish you can throw together in twenty minutes, but start a pot on Saturday afternoon and by sundown you'll have a spectacular, rib-sticking Tuscan supper.

Prepare the beans: Place the fresh beans in a pot and cover with 4 cups of cold water. In a piece of cheesecloth, tie the garlic cloves, sage, and peppercorns into a bundle and add to the beans. Bring to a very low simmer and cook until the beans are tender but not mushy, 20 to 30 minutes. Turn off the heat, stir in the salt and olive oil, and let cool to room temperature in the cooking liquid. Discard the cheesecloth bundle.

Make the Fagioli: Coat the bottom of a large skillet with the olive oil and heat over medium heat. Add the onion and sauté for 5 minutes. Add the garlic and pancetta, and sauté for another 3 to 4 minutes. Add the sage and crushed red pepper and cook for one more minute. Add the tomatoes and salt and pepper to taste, and cook for 10 minutes until a sauce begins to form.

Strain the beans, reserving the liquid. Add the beans to the tomato mixture and simmer uncovered for 20 minutes, adding some of the reserved bean cooking liquid (or water) if the mixture begins to look dry (it should be saucy). Taste for seasoning.

Make the Farrotto: Heat a large Dutch oven or skillet over medium heat. Add the olive oil and then the emmer. Stir for 3 minutes until the emmer is hot and has a nutty aroma.

Add 1 cup of bean cooking liquid (or stock or water), stirring occasionally until the liquid is absorbed, then add a second cup of liquid, stirring occasionally until it has also been absorbed, about 12 minutes total.

Add about two-thirds of the bean mixture, plus an additional 1 cup of bean cooking liquid (or stock or water) to the emmer. Cook about 5 to 8 minutes more, stirring occasionally, until the emmer is tender and almost all of the liquid is absorbed (add more liquid if the emmer is still too firm and the mixture is beginning to dry out). The mixture should be somewhat loose and saucy in texture, and the emmer should be tender but with a firm bite to the center.

Remove from heat and stir in the cheese, butter, and vinegar. Serve in shallow bowls with an extra spoonful of the cooked bean and tomato sauce over top.

SERVES 6 TO 8

Farrotto

¼ CUP EXTRA VIRGIN OLIVE OIL

1½ CUP UNCOOKED EMMER

3 CUPS LIQUID FROM COOKING BEANS, RESERVED FROM ABOVE (OR STOCK, WINE, OR WATER)

¾ CUP GRATED PARMESAN OR PECORINO CHEESE (OR ANY AGED GRATING CHEESE)

2 TABLESPOONS UNSALTED BUTTER

1 TABLESPOON RED WINE VINEGAR

ROASTED FINGERLING POTATOES WITH FRIED FARM EGG AND MISO MAYO

by **SEAN HELLER, MOMOFUKU NOODLE BAR**

Roasted Potatoes

1 POUND NUGGET OR FINGERLING POTATOES

2 TABLESPOONS SOY SAUCE

1 TABLESPOON LEMON JUICE

1 TABLESPOON SHERRY VINEGAR

¼ TEASPOON RED CHILI FLAKES

1 TABLESPOON VEGETABLE OIL

2 TABLESPOONS UNSALTED BUTTER, DICED INTO SMALL CUBES, DIVIDED

4 EGGS

SALT

¼ CUP HOISIN SAUCE, FOR SERVING

2 SCALLIONS, THINLY SLICED (WHITE AND GREEN PARTS), FOR SERVING

Miso Mayo

¼ CUP MAYONNAISE

3 TABLESPOONS SHIRO MISO

1 TEASPOON LEMON JUICE

2 TEASPOONS SHERRY VINEGAR

Leave it to the Momofuku team to turn the local harvest into an umami bomb. Here fingerling potatoes take on the powers of butter, soy sauce, sherry vinegar, and chili flakes, then cozy up to a rich miso mayo. As if that weren't rib-sticking enough, each plate is topped with a fried egg and hoisin sauce.

This recipe serves four, but if you're cooking for two, fry just two eggs, and set aside half the potatoes and miso mayo to reheat for a midnight snack or a breakfast of champions.

Rinse the potatoes, place in a large stockpot, cover with cold water, and season generously with salt. Bring to a boil over high heat, then reduce to a simmer and cook for about 15 minutes, or until a fork slides into a potato easily. Drain, let cool, and slice in half lengthwise.

Meanwhile make the miso mayo. In a mixing bowl, whisk together the mayonnaise, miso, lemon juice, and sherry vinegar. Set aside.

In a separate small bowl, whisk together the soy sauce, lemon juice, sherry vinegar, and red chili flakes.

Heat a 12-inch skillet over medium-high heat, add the vegetable oil, and then place the potatoes in the skillet, cut-side down. Reduce heat to medium and sear until golden brown, 4 to 5 minutes. Turn the potatoes to sear the other side, another 3 to 4 minutes. Reduce heat to low and add the soy–sherry vinegar–lemon juice mixture to deglaze the pan. Add 1 tablespoon butter, diced into 4 cubes. Use a rubber spatula to toss the potatoes with the glaze forming in the pan. Remove from the heat and cover to hold warm until ready to serve.

Heat a large skillet over medium heat. Add the remaining tablespoon of diced butter, and then crack the eggs into the pan. Sprinkle with a pinch of salt and reduce heat to low. Let sizzle, uncovered, for a minute, then continue to cook, covered, over low heat for 1 to 2 more minutes or until the egg white is set and the yolk is just warm and still wiggly.

To serve, place a smear of miso mayo on a plate, top with potatoes and a fried egg. Serve with a drizzle of hoisin sauce and the sliced scallions.

SERVES 4

GREEN TOMATO UPSIDE-DOWN CAKE

by MARK BITTMAN, *NEW YORK TIMES* COLUMNIST AND AUTHOR OF *HOW TO COOK EVERYTHING*

8 TABLESPOONS (1 STICK) MELTED, UNSALTED BUTTER, DIVIDED

½ CUP PACKED DARK BROWN SUGAR

2 LARGE, THICKLY SLICED GREEN TOMATOES, OR 3 SMALL

1 CUP BUTTERMILK

2 EGGS

½ CUP SUGAR

1½ CUPS ALL-PURPOSE FLOUR

½ CUP CORNMEAL

1 TEASPOON BAKING SODA

¼ TEASPOON SALT

Here that old classic, the pineapple upside-down cake, gets a locavore makeover that features green tomatoes. The fruit in question isn't those gorgeous Green Zebras or other green-when-ripe heirlooms. Rather, look for tomatoes that are as hard as potatoes, picked before sunshine and time on the vine render them tender, juicy, and red. Some farmers bring in a few green tomatoes all summer long, but they're most abundant each October when growers pick every last tomato before fall's first frost lays them to waste. That's the perfect time to make fried green tomatoes—or this unusual cake.

If you prefer to eat your tomatoes for dinner, not dessert, this cake is also fantastic with halved plums, sliced pears, rings of baking apples, or just about any other fruit in their place underneath the sticky caramel crown. At the holidays, cover the bottom of the pan with raw cranberries—out of the oven and inverted, they'll sparkle like rubies.

Preheat the oven to 350°F.

Liberally grease a 9-inch round cake pan or cast-iron skillet with half of the melted butter. Sprinkle the brown sugar evenly over the bottom of the pan and spread the tomatoes over in a single layer; set aside.

Whisk the remaining melted butter, buttermilk, eggs, and sugar together until foamy. In a separate bowl, combine the flour, cornmeal, baking soda, and salt. Gradually add the egg mixture to the flour mixture and stir until well incorporated.

Carefully spread the batter over the tomatoes, using a spatula to make sure it's evenly distributed. Bake until the top of the cake is golden brown and a toothpick inserted in the center comes out clean, 50 to 60 minutes. Let the cake cool in the pan for just 5 minutes.

Run a knife around the edge of the pan. Put the serving plate on the top of the cake pan and flip the pan and plate together so that the serving plate is now on the bottom and the cake pan is upside down and on top. The cake should fall out onto the serving plate. If the cake sticks, turn it right side up and run the knife along the edge again, then use a spatula to lift gently around the edge. Invert the cake again and tap on the bottom of the pan. If any of the tomatoes stick to the pan, don't worry; simply use a knife to remove the pieces and fill in any gaps on the top of the cake. Serve warm with whipped cream or ice cream.

MAKES ONE 9-INCH CAKE

Beekeeper DAVID GRAVES

BERKSHIRE BERRIES

David Graves doesn't seem like a law-breaking custom buster.

A soft-spoken man with a homespun stand, he's sold his family's jams, jellies, honey, and maple syrup for decades, and has been capturing nature's sweetness since before he lost his baby teeth. Back in 1956 when he was just six years old, he began helping his big brother tap sugar maples in their backyard in Williamsburg, Massachusetts, so you could say he was an old pro by the mid-1970s, when he and his wife, Mary, began selling their own preserves, including savory-sweet combinations such as Garlic Raspberry Jelly, Ginger Jelly, and Hot Strawberry Jam, from their front yard stand in western Massachusetts.

He still makes maple syrup the old-fashioned way, stockpiling logs all year and single-handedly collecting sap from eight hundred taps, which he boils around the clock each March on a wood-fired evaporator. "No reverse osmosis for me," he laughs.

He'll sell the syrup in small bottles all year long, alongside honey from his hives and the jams and jellies that Mary now makes with their daughter, Heather, from fruit they grow on their farm in the Berkshire Mountains. (Raspberry jam is the top seller, although his Berry Hot Garlic jelly spiked with jalapeño and homegrown garlic also has its followers. "I'm physiologically and psychologically addicted to the Berry Hot Garlic jelly," wrote one enthusiastic fan named Carly Simon. "I put it on rice cakes and lock myself in the closet and see no one for days.")

◀ *David's rooftop bees busily took to the Manhattan flora, collecting pollen from window boxes and flowering trees.* (Amanda Gentile)

Graves even does a brisk business with an almost-forgotten sweet-tart syrup called switchel that New England farmers long ago drank by the ladleful out in the hay and cornfields. His recipe, which calls only for ginger, raspberry vinegar, a touch of sugar, and well water, now provides traditional refreshment in the urban jungle.

But David's operation took a decidedly nontraditional turn in the 1990s.

It all began when black bears, hungry after hibernation, raided Graves's Massachusetts hives of their honey payload, and he experimented with elevating his remaining hives out of ursine reach. One day, sitting in traffic on the way to market, he looked up at the skyline and realized that there are no bears on city rooftops. An idea was born.

Back then it was illegal to keep honeybees in New York City; the health code banned bees as "wild, ferocious, fierce, dangerous, or naturally inclined to do harm." But Greenmarket founder Barry Benepe was intrigued by the idea, and in 1996 he allowed Graves to quietly set up a hive on the rooftop of the Greenmarket office on East 16th Street, two blocks east of Union Square.

The experimental urban apiary worked so well, Graves set out a sign at his stand, as if written by the bees: "We are very gentle. We like to share our New York City honey. Do you have a rooftop?"

Before long he sited a second hive, on 113th Street, and the rooftop project soon grew. He quickly developed rules (no fire escape hives, no ground-level hives, no wild roof parties, and all hives must be tied down or well weighted—it's windy up there.) By 1999, Graves was illicitly tending thirteen urban hives.

Like many New Yorkers, the bees are transplants—in this case, docile Italian honeybees shipped from a Georgia apiary—but they busily took to the Manhattan flora, collecting pollen and nectar from window boxes, parks, and the flowering trees that line so many city sidewalks. Linden, gingko, sumac, and black locust, along with a profusion of ornamental gardens, give the urban jars a more floral flavor than his clover-feeding Berkshire bees. Rooftop owners are "paid" with honey.

One day, sitting in traffic on the way to market, he looked up at the skyline and realized that there are no bears on city rooftops. An idea was born.

Thankfully the City's bee ban was overturned in 2010; there are now more than two hundred registered hives throughout the five boroughs. Graves still tends a half-dozen, aware that there aren't enough flowers in the city to nourish endless numbers of hives. But while his multistate operation—with a half-million bees, as well as an accompanying network of tenants, apartment owners, and landlords—may seem far removed from his early days, it all maintains the earnest feel of that 1970s front yard stand where locals slipped their payment into a wooden box and came back to return the jars, albeit with a city twist.

"Up in Massachusetts, I put hives on rooftops to keep them away from bears," laughs David. "Here I do it to keep to them away from people."

SPICED POUND CAKE WITH PEAR COMPOTE

By **MATT LEE AND TED LEE, AUTHORS OF** *THE LEE BROS. CHARLESTON KITCHEN*

Cake

1¾ CUPS SIFTED ALL-PURPOSE FLOUR, PLUS MORE FOR FLOURING THE PAN

½ TEASPOON BAKING SODA

½ TEASPOON SALT

½ TEASPOON GROUND GINGER

½ TEASPOON GROUND CINNAMON

¼ TEASPOON GROUND CAYENNE

4 WHOLE, LIGHTLY BEATEN EGGS

1½ TEASPOONS NATURAL VANILLA EXTRACT

1½ CUPS (2½ STICKS) UNSALTED BUTTER, SOFTENED, PLUS MORE FOR GREASING THE PAN

¾ CUP PLUS 2 TABLESPOONS LIGHT BROWN SUGAR

½ CUP WHOLE OR LOW-FAT BUTTERMILK

LIGHTLY SWEETENED WHIPPED CREAM (OPTIONAL)

You're going to be baking this recipe for years to come.

Yes, the classic pound cake proportions call for two and a half sticks of butter—but the Lee boys have added an alluring mixture of spices, including just one-quarter teaspoon of cayenne, which gives a whisper of warmth and suits the toffee flavors of the compote. Serve each slice with a generous spoonful of compote over the top so the cake will soak up the syrup.

Preheat the oven to 325°F.

Lightly grease and flour a 6-cup loaf pan.

Make the cake: In a medium bowl, sift the flour, baking soda, salt, and ground spices together twice.

In a measuring cup, whisk the eggs and vanilla together until thoroughly combined, about 1 minute.

In a large bowl, beat the butter with an electric mixer until creamy, about 30 seconds. Add the sugar and beat on high speed until the mixture is a maple-cream color and has a fluffy texture, about 2 minutes. Add the egg mixture in a thin stream and mix on slow speed about 2 minutes until it has been incorporated and the mixture has lightened in color and become smooth (it may look curdy, which is fine). Turn off the mixer and scrape down any batter that clings to the sides of the bowl.

Add the flour mixture in thirds, alternating with two ¼-cup additions of the buttermilk. To avoid overworking the batter, gently mix with a wooden spoon or rubber spatula after each addition until just incorporated.

Pour the batter into the pan and bake on the middle rack until a cake tester or toothpick inserted into the cake's center emerges clean, about 1 hour.

Make the compote: Pour the Madeira into a medium saucepan over medium heat, add the honey, salt, and cloves, and bring to a boil. Add the pears and ginger and cook until the pears are easily pierced with the tip of a knife, 6 to 10 minutes (depending on the ripeness of the pears).

With a slotted spoon, transfer the pears to a medium bowl and discard the cloves and ginger. Continue to cook the liquid over high heat until it has reduced by one-half, about 8 to 10 minutes (you should have 1 cup of liquid). It may not be syrupy, but it will thicken as it cools. Pour the syrup over the pears and let cool to room temperature. The compote will keep, covered, in the refrigerator for three days.

Remove the cake from the oven and let cool in its pan on a rack for about 15 minutes. Slide a thin knife around the edge of the pan and invert the cake onto a serving plate.

Serve slices of the cake warm with spoonfuls of the compote and dollops of whipped cream. Or let the cake cool completely on the rack, cover tightly with plastic wrap, and store at room temperature up to twenty-four hours. If storing longer, refrigerate for up to three days. If refrigerating the cake and compote, remember to remove it from the refrigerator 1 hour or more before serving to take the chill off.

MAKES 1 LOAF CAKE, SERVING 6 TO 8 PEOPLE

Compote

1½ CUPS MADEIRA, AMONTILLADO SHERRY, OR A FULL-BODIED WHITE WINE SUCH AS CHARDONNAY

⅓ CUP HONEY

¼ TEASPOON SALT

4 CLOVES

3 FIRM PEARS (ABOUT 1½ POUNDS), PEELED, CORED, AND DICED

1-INCH PIECE GRATED FRESH GINGER, PEELED, AND SLICED INTO COINS

Farmer KEN MIGLIORELLI
MIGLIORELLI FARM

Ken Migliorelli has one of the most diverse farms in New York, growing everything from cherries and peas to chard and pears. But while his stand looks like the cover of a seed catalog, his trademark crop isn't among the hundred-plus varieties of vegetables whose seeds he orders each winter. Instead that famous broccoli rabe is descended from heirloom seed his grandfather Angelo brought across the Atlantic when he immigrated to New York from the family's farm just south of Rome exactly one century ago.

Angelo first found work building the Holland Tunnel but soon got a job farming in the then-verdant fields of the Bronx. By 1933 he'd saved up enough money to buy his own land there, broke ground with a shovel, and built his own pushcart. The very first day he went out peddling produce he made almost ten bucks—back when many laborers made only one dollar a day. By year's end, he'd saved enough to buy a horse and an old "Drakes Cakes" wagon. He grew mostly greens—including that prized rabe from the mother country—as well as dandelion, escarole, and arugula other Italian immigrants hungered for, plus plum tomatoes, fennel, squash, and cucumbers. Slowly Angelo bought more land, and by the time he died in the 1950s, his son Rocco was tending the farm. (Rocco also peddled something else from a cart—hot dogs—which by then met a warmer reception than fennel and escarole.)

But just as Queens and Brooklyn were once the most productive agricultural counties in the nation, by

◀ *Ken Migliorelli grows nearly two hundred crops in the Hudson Valley, including a variety of broccoli rabe whose seeds his grandfather carried across the Atlantic a hundred years ago.* (Amanda Gentile)

the late 1960s the Bronx, too, became inhospitable to farming. In June of 1970, the Migliorelli family moved up to a dairy farm Angelo's other son had bought outside the Hudson Valley town of Red Hook.

The move was only one hundred miles, but for ten-year-old Ken, it felt like Angelo's immigration across continents. "I had never left the Bronx in my life," says Ken. "So going from there to here, it was culture shock." But his first night on the farm, the local farm kids gave him a bovine baptism—walking barefoot through manure. "I loved it," remembers Ken.

Ken's grandfather Angelo farmed in the Bronx, mostly growing the rabe, escarole, and arugula other Italian immigrants hungered for.

Soon, Ken, in the spirit of his grandfather, would fill his little red wagon with cucumbers and walk half a mile to a housing development where he sold them door to door. (The rest of the family's vegetables went to wholesale markets at Hunts Point and in Albany.)

Ken is quick to point out that his mother, Benita, and grandmother, Concetta, worked at least as hard as the men. "My mom worked a full-time job in the hospital," marvels Ken, "came home, and worked in the fields, had dinner on the table at six, and the house was always clean." But the farm struggled financially for years.

In 1981, back from studying agronomy and agricultural business at SUNY-Cobleskill, Ken went over the family's books and realized the farm was nearly thirty

thousand dollars in debt—and losing more money every season. "I looked at my parents and said, 'I love farming,'" he recalls, "'but we can't continue like this.'"

For years, a friend of his mother's had been suggesting, "Why don't you go to these Greenmarkets in the city?" So Ken finally called up, talked with Greenmarket cofounder Barry Benepe for an hour, and soon was scheduled to sell at three city markets.

His first day at market wasn't quite the economic equivalent of Angelo's inaugural day, but he sold pretty much the same produce—tomatoes, squash, fennel, cucumbers, and plenty of Italian greens. Spanish Harlem was his best market. "At the end of that first year," he remembers, satisfaction still in his voice, "we had paid bills we owed from '80 and '81. For me, it made farming promising."

As they made a living, the farm expanded, and they left the clay soil for flat loamy acres next door. Like his grandfather, Ken added land in bits and pieces, even annexing a 200-acre orchard in 2002. Today he owns 400 acres, rents additional land from eight different parties, and all in, cultivates a thousand acres.

Ken's mom still takes care of the farm checkbook, his daughter, Carly, and her husband work on the farm, and his younger daughter Chelsea is studying plant science at Cobleskill; last fall she had three of the same professors who had taught her dad. Just like Ken, his kids see a future on the farm.

Back on that first day at Greenmarket, the farm grew about 40 different crops; today that tally is up over 180—from Romano beans to tomatillos to 20 varieties of apples. But Angelo's broccoli rabe is still a top seller, each bunch hand-tied in twine. Those seeds have covered a lot of ground over the last century. Thanks to multiple Migliorellis, thousands of New Yorkers eat as well as Ken's ancestors did back in Italy.

POACHED QUINCE

by **PETER HOFFMAN, BACK FORTY AND BACK FORTY WEST**

1½ CUP NEW YORK STATE
OFF-DRY RIESLING

¾ CUP SUGAR

3 TABLESPOONS LEMON JUICE,
FROM ABOUT 1 LEMON

4 MEDIUM QUINCE, PEELED,
CORED, AND QUARTERED

Appearing at orchard stands in October, quince has the look of a fuzzy apple—and the aroma of a ripe pineapple. Quite hard and tart, the fruit is seldom eaten raw, but once roasted, baked or, in this case, poached, it will turn tender, sweet, and rose pink. Serve cooked quince over yogurt, ice cream, cake, or pancakes. And save the poaching liquid—if you pour it, still warm, into a small container, it will solidify, once chilled, into a locavore version of what the Spanish call *membrillo*—and serve alongside aged cheese.

In a large stockpot, combine the wine, sugar, and lemon juice with 2 cups of water and bring to a simmer over medium heat. Stir to dissolve the sugar.

Add the quince, return to a simmer, and then reduce the heat to low, just under the simmer point, to very gently poach the quince without any agitating bubbles. After about 1 hour of cooking the quince will be tender and delicious, but I prefer to cook them even longer, for a total of three to four hours. The yellow flesh will slowly become rose colored and then take on a deep vermillion, with a velvety soft texture that maintains its shape. Take it as far as you like or have time for.

Remove the quince from the heat and serve warm or let cool to room temperature. Poached quince can be stored in its cooking liquid in the refrigerator for up to two weeks.

APPLE VERMOUTH

by **AUDREY SAUNDERS, PEGU CLUB**

6 MACINTOSH APPLES, CORED AND THINLY SLICED

1 LITER NOILLY PRAT DRY VERMOUTH

"This is one of my favorite infusions!" So writes mixologist Audrey Saunders, whose Pegu Club on Houston Street is widely credited for the cocktail renaissance.

The libation could hardly be easier to make. Simply slice Macintosh apples— "I tried eight different varieties," she says, "and none were nearly as good as Mac"—cover with vermouth, and refrigerate, shaking daily as it infuses.

Saunders enjoys it straight or mixed into cocktails. "At first sip it tastes like a lively cider," she writes. "And then as it warms up, a wonderful complexity from the vermouth begins to express itself."

"Warning," she concludes, "this infusion is fairly insidious and quite easy to drink in quantity."

Combine the apple slices and vermouth in a 1.5-liter container with a lid (a canning jar of this size works perfectly).

Close the lid and gently shake for 10 to 15 seconds.

Cold-infuse the mixture in the refrigerator for 5 days, shaking once daily.

On the fifth day, remove from the fridge, strain, and discard the apples. Store the infusion in the refrigerator.

MAKES 1 LITER

BOSC PEAR

MACOUN

SECKEL PEAR

IDA RED

HONEY
CRISP

PINK LADY

MACOUN

MUTSU

BOSC PEAR

LACK TWIG

SECKEL
PEAR

BOSC PEAR

WINTER
BANANA

BLACK TWIG

BOSC PEAR

MACOUN

Winter

ABC WINTER SALAD

by **JOAN GUSSOW, AUTHOR OF** *THIS ORGANIC LIFE*

1 LARGE APPLE, CORED

2 MEDIUM PEELED BEETS

2 LARGE CARROTS

1 TABLESPOON FRESHLY GRATED GINGER

JUICE OF 1 LIME OR LEMON, OR HALF OF AN ORANGE

1 TO 2 TABLESPOONS OLIVE OIL

SALT AND PEPPER TO TASTE

¼ CUP THINLY SLICED SCALLIONS, FOR GARNISH (OPTIONAL)

¼ CUP WALNUTS FOR GARNISH (OPTIONAL)

Cold weather makes us crave burbling stews and slow roasts. But nutritionist Joan Gussow—a Columbia University professor who has been fighting for a return to a farm-based food system for fifty years—knows that sometimes you just need a salad. And while one locavore named winter "the leafless season," Gussow's simple slaw of grated raw apple, beets, and carrots is a bright delight on the darkest days of the year. The citrus and ginger make it so refreshing, you'll find yourself craving it in summer, too.

Using a grater or the grating attachment of a food processor, shred the apples, beets, and carrots.

In a large mixing bowl, combine the ginger, citrus juice, olive oil, salt, and pepper.

Add the grated mixture and toss to combine. Season to taste with salt and pepper. If desired, serve topped with scallions and walnuts.

SERVES 4

SPICED SQUASH SOUP

by **JEREMY BEARMAN, ROUGE TOMATE**

1 TABLESPOON OLIVE OIL

½ CUP DICED CARROT, FROM
ABOUT 1 MEDIUM CARROT

½ CUP DICED CELERY, FROM
ABOUT 1 CELERY RIB

1 CUP DICED ONION, FROM ABOUT
1 ONION

4 TO 5 CUPS WINTER SQUASH,
IDEALLY A MIX OF BUTTERNUT AND
KABOCHA, PEELED, AND CUT INTO
1-INCH CUBES (RESERVE SEEDS
FOR GARNISH, SEE NOTE ON
PAGE 166)

2 WHOLE CLOVES

½ TEASPOON BLACK PEPPERCORNS

½ TEASPOON STAR ANISE

2 STICKS CINNAMON

2 TO 3 CUPS VEGETABLE STOCK OR
WATER

1½ CUPS WHOLE MILK

SALT AND PEPPER TO TASTE

MAPLE SYRUP, OPTIONAL, TO TASTE

Garnish Ideas

½ CUP DICED APPLE, SAUTÉED
IN A LITTLE BUTTER

¼ CUP TOASTED PUMPKIN SEEDS

4 TEASPOONS PUMPKIN SEED OIL

Containing no butter or cream, this simple, healthful soup is both comforting and clean-tasting. The cinnamon, star anise, and black pepper channel the aromas of chai, but the squash's own flavor shines through. You can use any variety, but kabocha, which is widely available at farmers markets and sometimes called Japanese pumpkin, is sweeter and more flavorful than the acorn or butternut you grew up on. A little drizzle of maple syrup turns up the sweetness just a touch.

In a large pot, warm the olive oil over medium heat, then sweat the carrot, celery, onion, and squash until soft but not browned, 10 to 15 minutes.

Combine the spices in a cheesecloth sachet and add to the pot with the stock or water; continue to cook until all vegetables are tender. The vegetables need to be completely cooked so they are easily pureed.

Take off the heat, remove the sachet, add the milk, and puree in batches until smooth. Check the seasoning and add maple syrup for extra sweetness if you like.

Serve warm, garnished with sautéed apple, toasted pumpkin seeds, and/or a drizzle of pumpkin seed oil.

SERVES 4 TO 6

KABOCHA

DELICATA

CALABAZA

SWEET MEAT

GOLDEN HUBBARD

CARNIVAL

CELERY ROOT AND SUNCHOKE SOUP

by **STEVEN LINARES, FORT DEFIANCE**

2½ POUNDS SUNCHOKES

1¼ POUNDS CELERY ROOT
(ABOUT 1 LARGE OR 2 MEDIUM-
SIZED BULBS), PEELED WITH
A KNIFE

¼ POUND PEELED PARSNIPS
(ABOUT 1 MEDIUM PARSNIP)

¼ POUND FENNEL (ABOUT HALF
A SMALL BULB)

⅓ POUND SMALL WHITE TURNIPS,
PREFERABLY HAKUREI

4 TABLESPOONS (HALF A STICK)
UNSALTED BUTTER

2 TEASPOON SALT

2 CUPS HALF AND HALF

WALNUT OIL AND/OR MAPLE
SYRUP, TO DRIZZLE

Before the advent of the heated greenhouse, winter vegetables came from one place: the root cellar. After the fall harvest, farmers filled basements and burrows with potatoes, beets, carrots, and other starchy-sweet things that grow underground and keep families well fed all winter long. When even the kale and Brussels sprouts are a memory, you can simmer up this simple soup of flavorful roots. Even if you use only one cup of half and half, the result is a lusciously comforting velvet puree.

Thinly slice all the vegetables. They'll be pureed later so don't worry about perfection; you just want them to cook evenly.

In a large pot, melt the butter over medium heat, then add the vegetables and salt and cook until the vegetables start to release their liquid and are soft, about 30 minutes.

Add the half and half and 4 cups of water, return to a low simmer, and cook for 10 minutes or until the vegetables can be easily mashed with a fork. Transfer to a blender, in batches if necessary, and puree on high for a full minute. Serve hot, with a drizzle of walnut oil and maple syrup.

SERVES 8 AS AN APPETIZER, 4 AS A MAIN

CRISPY DUCK BREAST WITH KALE, TUR[N]
AND BLOOD ORANGE SAUCE

by **CHARLES RODRIGUEZ, PRINT. RESTAURANT**

Small farmers and home cooks alike are slowly discovering what great chefs have long known: that duck for dinner means excellent flavor, luxurious fat, and spectacularly crisp skin. This dish is a play on the French classic Duck à l'Orange; winter's blood oranges offer a dramatic hue on the plate, but you could also use the fresh juice of navel oranges. Braised turnips and kale counterbalance all that lip-smacking richness and sweetness.

Be sure to save every drop of rendered duck fat. It keeps for at least a month in the fridge, and will make the best roasted potatoes you've ever tasted.

1 CUP BLOOD ORANGE JUICE (FROM ABOUT 8 BLOOD ORANGES)

2 POUNDS BONELESS, SKIN-ON DUCK BREASTS (ABOUT 4 DUCK BREASTS)

1 POUND BABY TURNIPS LEFT UNPEELED, OR LARGE TURNIPS PEELED, CUT INTO 1-INCH DICE

¾ CUP CHICKEN OR VEGETABLE STOCK, DIVIDED

1 BUNCH LACINATO KALE, STEMS REMOVED, SLICED CROSSWISE INTO THIN, ¼-INCH THICK STRIPS

SALT AND FRESHLY GROUND BLACK PEPPER

Make the sauce: In a small saucepan over medium-low heat, reduce the blood orange juice to a syrup, or until you end up with ¼ cup, about 12 to 15 minutes. Remove from heat and set aside.

Cook the duck: With the tip of a paring knife, score the skin of the duck breasts in a cross-hatch or diamond pattern, with the lines ½-inch apart, being careful not to touch the flesh with the knife, only the skin and fat. Season both sides well with salt and pepper.

Heat a large sauté pan over medium-low heat, then add the duck breasts, skin side down, and cook until the skin becomes golden and crispy, 12 to 15 minutes, periodically pouring out the rendered fat into a small bowl. Turn the duck and cook on the other side for 3 minutes for rare, 4 to 5 minutes for medium rare. Remove the breasts from the pan and let them rest on a cutting board while you prepare the turnips and kale.

(continued) ▶

Remove all but 1 tablespoon of duck fat from the pan. Add the turnips, ½ cup of stock, and a pinch of salt. Bring to a simmer, then reduce heat to low and braise the turnips, partially covered, for 10 to 12 minutes, or until slightly tender but not mushy. Remove the turnips and set aside.

Remove any remaining stock and return the dry pan to medium heat. Add 1 tablespoon of the reserved duck fat, the kale, the remaining ¼ cup of stock, and a pinch of salt and pepper. Bring to a simmer and cook, partially covered, for 3 to 4 minutes, or until the kale wilts. Remove the lid and continue to cook until the liquid cooks off, about 2 more minutes. Return the turnips to the pan.

Slice the duck crosswise into ½-inch thick slices and serve over the kale and turnips, finish with a drizzle of blood orange sauce and a sprinkle of salt.

SERVES 4

GARGANELLI AL CONIGLIO

by **NICK ANDERER, MAIALINO**

Braised Rabbit

3 POUNDS RABBIT (LEGS ONLY, IF AVAILABLE, OR ONE WHOLE 3-POUND RABBIT)

1 TABLESPOON OLIVE OIL

6 OUNCES PROSCIUTTO TRIMMINGS OR PANCETTA, CUT INTO 2-INCH CUBES

5 SMASHED GARLIC CLOVES

1 CUP MEDIUM-DICE SHALLOT, FROM ABOUT 3 LARGE SHALLOTS

1 QUART CHICKEN STOCK

2 SPRIGS ROSEMARY

1 TEASPOON CHILI FLAKES

2 BAY LEAVES

1 TEASPOON WHOLE PEPPERCORNS

½ TEASPOON SALT

Danny Meyer called his Gramercy Park trattoria after the nickname he earned as a young man in Rome, where "Meyerlino" (little Meyer) sounded an awful lot like his favorite dish, maialino (roast suckling pig).

Today, Meyer's Roman menu serves pork aplenty—but eaters in the know order Chef Anderer's coniglio.

Many Americans who eat pork and beef all day put down their forks at the thought of anything petlike. But rabbit deserves a place on the plate. Natural herbivores, they grow quickly on nothing but grass and reproduce like, well, you know. Beyond sustainability, they're excellent eating: The meat is silky and succulent, especially in this warming winter ragù. Make it once, and even when not in Rome you'll want to do as the Romans do.

If using a whole rabbit, remove the legs. Break down the backbone including the pelvis, belly, and breast into four large pieces.

Preheat the oven to 375°F.

Braise the rabbit: Place a large Dutch oven over medium-low heat. Add 1 tablespoon olive oil and the prosciutto and cook slowly to render out all of the fat, about 10 to 12 minutes. Add the garlic and shallot, and sweat at a low heat until translucent, about 5 to 7 more minutes. Add the chicken stock, rabbit pieces, rosemary, chili flakes, bay leaves, peppercorns, and salt, and increase heat to medium high. Bring just to a simmer, then cover with a lid and transfer to the oven. Braise until the meat is tender and falling off the bone, about 35 to 40 minutes. Remove the rabbit pieces from the pot and set aside until cool enough to handle, then remove only the flesh from the bones, discarding the skin and other tendons. Strain the braising liquid, discarding solids and reserving the liquid.

Complete the pasta dish: Bring a large pot of water to a boil. Season generously with salt to taste like the ocean.

Wipe out the Dutch oven and return to medium-low heat. Add the remaining 1 tablespoon of olive oil, then the garlic. Toast the garlic for about 2 minutes. Turn off the heat and add the rosemary to the warm oil, stirring for 1 minute.

Return the rabbit-braising liquid to the Dutch oven and place over medium heat. Simmer until reduced by half, about 15 to 20 minutes. Once reduced, add the crushed tomatoes and pulled meat, and continue to simmer over low heat.

Meanwhile, cook the pasta according to the package directions, until al dente. Reserve ¼ cup of the pasta water and strain the pasta. Add the cooked pasta, pasta water, butter, and cheese to the braising liquid and continue to stir and simmer over medium heat for 1 to 2 minutes, until the pasta is tender and the sauce coats the pasta. Remove the garlic cloves and finish with parsley, lemon juice, and vinegar.

SERVES 4

Pasta

1 TABLESPOON OLIVE OIL

3 WHOLE GARLIC CLOVES

1 TABLESPOON CHOPPED ROSEMARY

⅔ CUP CANNED CRUSHED TOMATOES

1 POUND GARGANELLI PASTA

2 TABLESPOONS UNSALTED BUTTER

1 CUP FINELY GRATED GRANA PADANO CHEESE

2 TABLESPOONS CHOPPED PARSLEY

2 TABLESPOONS LEMON JUICE, FROM ABOUT 1 LEMON

2 TEASPOONS CHAMPAGNE VINEGAR

PECONIC BAY SCALLOPS WITH GINGER-LIME MARINIÈRE

by **ERIC RIPERT, LE BERNARDIN**

Mussel Stock

1 TABLESPOON CANOLA OIL

1 LARGE SHALLOT, PEELED AND THINLY SLICED, ABOUT ¼ CUP

2 GARLIC CLOVES, PEELED AND THINLY SLICED, ABOUT 1 TABLESPOON

½ CUP WHITE WINE

3 POUNDS MUSSELS, CLEANED AND BEARDS PULLED OFF

Much smaller and sweeter than more common sea scallops, bay scallops are a delicacy that grow tiny and tender in the Great Peconic Bay on the East End of Long Island and are harvested November through March.

This recipe is simple enough for the home cook, but it's haute cuisine, truly tasting as though it were made by a Michelin-starred chef, with the ginger and lime giving a distinct Vietnamese flavor.

A few notes: Chef Ripert makes a simple mussel stock but doesn't use the mussel meat in the dish; cover the cooked mussels with any extra stock and use or freeze within a day or two. They're great tossed into pasta. And no, we didn't omit a step here—the scallops aren't actually cooked, but merely warmed. It's sublime.

Make the stock: In a medium stockpot over medium heat, combine the canola oil, shallot, and garlic and sweat until softened but not browned, about 1½ minutes. Add the wine and bring to a simmer. Add the mussels and cook, covered, over medium heat until all of the mussels have opened and the liquid has been cooked out of them, 8 to 10 minutes, stirring once midway through. With a slotted spoon, remove the mussels and discard the shells, reserving the mussel meat for another use. Strain the remaining stock through a fine mesh sieve. Cool the stock and refrigerate for up to three days, or freeze for up to two months.

Preheat the oven to 350°F.

Trim the root end of the leeks and cut off the fibrous dark green top, leaving only the white and light green part of the leeks. Cut in half lengthwise and rinse well under cold water. Slice into strips about ⅛-inch thick.

Heat ¼ cup of water and 1 tablespoon of butter in a sauté pan. Add the leeks and a pinch of salt and cook on low heat until tender, about 15 minutes, adding a little water if the leeks become dry. Keep warm.

Meanwhile, heat a small stockpot over medium-low heat and add 1 teaspoon of canola oil. Sweat the garlic and shallots until translucent, about 5 minutes. Add the mussel stock to the pot and bring to a simmer. Simmer for about 10 minutes then turn off the heat and add the lime leaf and ginger and steep, covered, for another 10 minutes to infuse the flavors. Strain into a small pot. Add the lime juice, adjust the seasoning, and keep warm.

For the Scallops: Line a sheet pan with parchment paper and brush with the remaining teaspoon of canola oil. Place the scallops on the pan and season with salt, pepper, and Piment d'Espelette. Place into the oven for 1 minute to warm gently.

Plate the leeks and slice the scallops in half crosswise and arrange cut-side up on top of the leeks. Grate a few flecks of fresh lime zest over them.

Return the sauce to a simmer and whisk in the remaining 2 tablespoons of butter. Pour the warm sauce over and around the scallops and serve.

SERVES 4

Scallops

2 LEEKS

3 TABLESPOONS COLD BUTTER, DIVIDED

2 TEASPOONS CANOLA OIL, DIVIDED

2 GARLIC CLOVES, PEELED AND THINLY SLICED

2 SHALLOTS, PEELED AND THINLY SLICED

1½ CUPS MUSSEL STOCK (RECIPE ABOVE)

1 FRESH KAFFIR LIME LEAF (OPTIONAL)

1 LIME

1 2-INCH PIECE OF GINGER, PEELED AND THINLY SLICED

32 PECONIC BAY SCALLOPS

FINE SEA SALT

FRESHLY GROUND WHITE PEPPER

PIMENT D'ESPELETTE

WINE-BRINED BRISKET

by JIMMY CARBONE, JIMMY'S NO. 43

Brine

1 CUP SALT

1 CUP SUGAR

1 BAY LEAF

1 SLICED ONION

Beef

2 TABLESPOONS VEGETABLE OIL, DIVIDED

4 POUND CUT OF BRISKET, RUMP, OR SHOULDER

2 THICKLY SLICED ONIONS

3 LARGE CARROTS, PEELED, HALVED LENGTHWISE AND CUT INTO 2-INCH PIECES

1 BOTTLE RED WINE, PREFERABLY FINGER LAKES PINOT NOIR OR AN INDIGENOUS GRAPE BLEND SUCH AS THIRSTY OWL LOT 99

1 TABLESPOON WHOLE GRAIN OR DIJON MUSTARD

Every winter Jimmy's No. 43 in the East Village hosts a brisket cook-off, and owner Jimmy Carbone has picked up a few tricks. One, cribbed from BBQ pros, is that a long, slow cook transforms the cut from tough to tender.

But the real secret here is the red-wine brine. Yes, you have to begin three days in advance, but the brine is very simple to stir together and infuses the meat with great flavor—something between a pot roast and a corned beef. Don't skip the sharp mustard whisked in at the end.

To brine the beef: In a large pot, combine the salt, sugar, bay leaf, and onion and cover with 2 quarts of water. Bring to a boil and stir until the sugar and salt dissolve. Remove from heat. When fully cooled, transfer to a 3-quart container or plastic bag and place the beef in it. Make sure that the liquid covers the beef completely. Marinate the beef for forty-eight hours in the brine. After two days, discard the brine and pat the beef dry with paper towels. Let it rest in the refrigerator, uncovered, for one more day to fully dry out.

To braise the beef: Preheat the oven to 300°F.

Heat one tablespoon of vegetable oil in a large Dutch oven over medium-high heat. Sear the beef on all sides until golden brown, about 5 minutes per side (if the beef does not lay flat to sear in the Dutch oven, it can be seared in a large sauté pan, then transferred to the Dutch oven to braise). Remove the beef and set aside. Wipe out the pot, add the remaining one tablespoon of oil, then the onions and carrots. Cook until golden, 5 to 7 minutes. Add the red wine, bring to a simmer, and scrape up any brown bits from the bottom of the pan. Return the beef to the pot, cover with the lid, and place in the oven for 4 hours.

After 4 hours, remove the meat from the pot and let rest, covered, while you make the pan gravy. Remove the onions and carrots from the pot (and eat them if you like!). Heat the remaining liquid in the Dutch oven over med-high heat to reduce, skimming the fat from the surface frequently. Reduce by two-thirds, about 12 to 15 minutes. Once reduced, turn off the heat and whisk in the mustard. Adjust the seasoning with salt and pepper (it won't need much salt, as the brine will provide enough seasoning).

Slice the beef and serve with the sauce and roasted or boiled fingerling potatoes.

SERVES 4 TO 6

ROASTED SAUSAGE WITH RIESLING CABBAGE

By **KURT GUTENBRUNNER, WALLSÉ**

1 TABLESPOON OLIVE OIL

1 PEELED AND DICED ONION

1 TEASPOON SALT

1 HEAD WHITE CABBAGE, ABOUT
2 POUNDS, CORED AND THINLY
SLICED

1 CUP RIESLING WINE

1 TABLESPOON CARAWAY SEEDS

1 TABLESPOON WHITE WINE
VINEGAR

8 BRATWURST SAUSAGES

SALT AND FRESHLY GROUND
BLACK PEPPER

This warming winter dish can be made on even the darkest night when fields are frozen and the cupboard is bare. While cabbage and onion simmer on the stovetop, sausage in the oven is hands-off and splatter-free. The floral, high-acid Riesling channels Chef Gutenbrunner's Austrian roots, but we recommend a bottle from New York's award-winning Finger Lakes wine region.

To make this richer, toss the pan drippings over the cabbage and cut the extra unctuousness with a grated tart apple or an extra squeeze of lemon.

Preheat the oven to 400°F.

In a large stockpot over medium heat, heat the olive oil and swirl to coat the bottom of the pan. Add the onion, season with 1 teaspoon of salt, and sweat until soft and translucent, about 5 minutes. Add the cabbage and stir to combine. Continue to sweat, stirring occasionally, 5 more minutes. Increase heat to high and add the wine. Bring to a simmer and season with salt, pepper, and caraway seeds. Reduce heat to low, cover, and braise for 30 minutes. Adjust the seasoning and finish with the vinegar.

Meanwhile pat the sausages dry with a paper towel and place them in a roasting pan. Roast in the oven for 15 to 20 minutes, turning once to brown each side. The internal temperature should read 165°F. Let rest for 5 minutes and serve with the cabbage.

SERVES 4 TO 6

Farmer MICHAEL GRADY ROBERTSON

SAWKILL FARM

While most Greenmarket farmers are passing through middle age, others are fresh-faced twenty-year-olds—the second, third, or even seventh generation to work their family's land. Michael Grady Robertson doesn't fit into either category. Instead he's a part of the growing phenomenon of young people trading office jobs for agriculture.

Growing up in the Kansas City suburbs, he never gave farming a moment's thought, and after graduating from college during the Internet boom, he made good money at dot-com jobs in Austin. But he hated sitting at a desk all day while the computer screen made his eyes water, and in 2004, in his mid-twenties, he quit.

Still, he needed to pay the rent, and when an organic vegetable farm that sold at the Austin farmers market posted a job opening in the local paper, he thought it sounded better than another sentence in a cubicle. Soon he was hand weeding all day under the Texas sun. He was the slowest member of the crew, and sometimes fire ants crawled up his pants, but he loved being outside and realized he felt at home in a world he'd never known existed.

After some travel he landed in New York and applied for a position at Hawthorne Valley Farm in the Hudson Valley. While learning the animal side of agriculture—from grass-fed dairy and beef to pastured chicken and pigs—he researched job possibilities and came across a place called Queens County Farm

◀ *Growing up in the suburbs, Michael never gave agriculture a moment's thought. But when an organic farm posted a job opening, he thought it sounded better than a cubicle.*

Museum. A historic piece of land owned by the New York City Department of Parks and Recreation, the property was open to the public, but its "farm" was little more than a few ancient apple trees, a petting zoo, and a candy shop. Robertson proposed to turn the sleepy project into a model farm, and he landed the job.

True to his word, he spent two years transforming Queens County Farm into a vibrant demonstration of sustainable agriculture, right in the city, complete with fields of heirloom vegetables and heritage-breed hogs lolling under trees, while 747s from nearby LaGuardia Airport roared overhead. QCF applied to sell at Greenmarket, and soon New Yorkers were buying chard and carrots grown on a farm they could take a taxi to.

Meanwhile Robertson was looking for land and eventually found his dream spot in Red Hook, New York: 65 acres with good water and great soil, complete with a conservation easement that brought down the price and ensures that the farm can never be sold for development.

Less than a decade after first learning to weed, Robertson now brings his own vegetables to market but is best known for his pastured chicken, woods-raised pork, and grass-fed, grass-finished beef and lamb.

In the years since he left office life, thousands of young people nationwide have followed a similar path from suburbia and college out onto farms, drawn to ecological agriculture instead of digital ad sales or search engine optimization. Robertson is something of a trailblazing success story, but at thirty-eight, he laughs that he's not sure he qualifies for the term "young farmer" any longer. When it comes to that category, "I'm like Justin Timberlake," he jokes. "An elder statesman."

Less than a decade after learning to weed, Michael is known for his free-range chicken and pastured pork.

BUCKWHEAT HONEY ROASTED LAMB RIBS WITH FINGERLING POTATO SALAD

by **FATTY CRAB**

Lamb

2 BONE-IN LAMB BREASTS, ABOUT 2 POUNDS

3 TABLESPOONS BUCKWHEAT HONEY

2 TABLESPOONS BROWN RICE VINEGAR

2 TEASPOONS TURMERIC POWDER

2 TABLESPOONS WHOLE CORIANDER SEED, LIGHTLY TOASTED AND CRACKED IN A MORTAR AND PESTLE

Potatoes

1 POUND FINGERLING POTATOES

2 GARLIC CLOVES

2 TABLESPOONS WHOLE BLACK PEPPERCORNS

3 BAY LEAVES

½ CUP YOGURT

1 TABLESPOON LIME JUICE, FROM ABOUT 1 LIME

2 TABLESPOONS CHOPPED SHALLOTS

SALT AND FRESHLY GROUND BLACK PEPPER

This unusual winter dish could hardly be easier. Simply stick a whole rack of lamb ribs in the oven until the meat is tender and the crust is caramelized and crispy. In typical Fatty Crab style, the flavorful baste, brushed on for the final few minutes, channels the Southeast Asian pantry. Lamb ribs are a little fattier than pork ribs, so eat them before they get cold, with or without the yogurt-kissed potato salad, which is so bright and tangy you'll want to make it year-round. Come spring, swap in chives for the shallots.

Preheat the oven to 400°F.

Season the lamb breast with salt and place on a metal roasting rack with a tray underneath. Roast for 90 minutes or until fork tender and golden brown. Meanwhile, whisk together the honey, vinegar, turmeric, and coriander seed. During the last 10 minutes of cooking, baste the lamb on both sides with the honey mixture and return to the oven.

While the lamb cooks, place the potatoes in a medium pot and cover with cold water. Smash the garlic with the back of a knife and add to the potatoes along with the peppercorns, bay leaves, and a generous amount of salt. Bring the potatoes to a simmer and cook until fork tender, about 25 minutes. Drain the potatoes and, when cool, slice into ½-inch coins and dress in the yogurt, lime juice, chopped shallots, black pepper, and salt.

After the 90 minutes, remove the lamb from the oven and baste again. Let rest 10 minutes. To serve, slice the lamb into individual ribs and drizzle with any of the honey mixture that has dripped off. Serve the potato salad on the side.

SERVES 2 TO 4

CIDER-BRAISED PORK SHOULDER [OR BUTT] WITH ONIONS

by **MIKE YEZZI, FLYING PIGS FARM**

Start this cold-weather classic early in the afternoon, and relax while the appley aroma fills your home. The pork's internal temperature should reach 160°F, but don't worry if it climbs higher—it is almost impossible to overcook this cut. Alternatively, you can braise it in a slow cooker instead of the oven.

Serve the shredded pork over creamy polenta or alongside potatoes, with plenty of the cidery sauce spooned over top.

1 3- TO 4-POUND PORK BONE-IN SHOULDER OR BONELESS BUTT

2 THINLY SLICED GARLIC CLOVES

1 TABLESPOON VEGETABLE OIL

1½ POUNDS THINLY SLICED ONIONS, ABOUT 4 MEDIUM ONIONS

1½ CUPS APPLE CIDER

SALT AND FRESHLY GROUND BLACK PEPPER

Preheat the oven to 325°F.

With a sharp knife, cut 1-inch deep slits all over the pork. Insert a slice of garlic completely into each slit. Pat dry and season with salt and pepper.

Heat the oil in a 4- to 5-quart ovenproof heavy pot or Dutch oven over medium-high heat until hot but not smoking. Reduce heat to medium and sear the pork until golden brown, 2 minutes per side. Rest on a plate.

Add the onions and sauté over low heat, stirring occasionally, until golden brown, 10 to 15 minutes. Add ¾ teaspoon of salt.

Add the cider, bring to a boil, then lower the heat to simmer. Return the pork to the pot, fat side up, cover with a lid and transfer to the oven. Braise, turning once, until falling apart, about 3 hours.

Transfer the pork to a cutting board or rimmed baking sheet and let rest until cool enough to handle. Meanwhile, strain the onions from the cooking liquid into a tall, narrow container and let the fat rise to the top. Spoon off most of the fat and discard; return the liquid and onions to the pot. Using two forks or your hands, pull the pork from the bone, return to the pot, season with salt and pepper, and serve.

This pork can be made a day or two in advance and reheated.

SERVES 6 TO 8

VEAL CHOP WITH BRAISED VEGETABLES

by **ROBERT NEWTON, SEERSUCKER**

Braised Vegetables

2 TABLESPOONS EXTRA VIRGIN OLIVE OIL

2 CLOVES MINCED GARLIC

1 PINCH RED CHILI FLAKES

6 SPRIGS THYME

8 OUNCES FINGERLING POTATOES, CLEANED AND SLICED IN HALF LENGTHWISE

4 OUNCES JERUSALEM ARTICHOKES, CLEANED AND SLICED INTO ½-INCH COINS

4 OUNCES SMALL CARROTS, PEELED AND SLICED IN HALF LENGTHWISE

2 CUPS CHICKEN STOCK

1 TABLESPOON DICED, UNSALTED BUTTER

1 TABLESPOON LEMON JUICE, FROM ABOUT ½ LEMON

SALT

Veal

2 8- TO 10-OUNCE BONE-IN VEAL CHOPS

SALT AND FRESHLY GROUND BLACK PEPPER

1 TABLESPOON CHOPPED THYME

1 TABLESPOON CHOPPED ROSEMARY

1 TABLESPOON EXTRA VIRGIN OLIVE OIL

Veal at Greenmarket is what you'd call a different animal. Raised not in tiny indoor pens but out on greener pastures, the calves lead a good life. And while the young meat is tender, that outdoor exercise means muscle tone rather than mush.

But there's another reason to seek out local veal: The Northeast is known for dairy, and all those milkers give birth yearly. Half of their babies are bull calves traditionally sold at auction for pennies a pound. When those animals can instead be raised right and sold as "baby beef," it's better for them, the farmers, and us eaters, too. For these reasons, Chef Rob only uses veal from Consider Bardwell Farm, which sells at the Carroll Gardens Greenmarket right across the street from his restaurant. The veal cooks up quickly, just three to four minutes per side.

Preheat the oven to 350°F.

Make the vegetables: Heat a medium saucepan over medium heat. Add the olive oil, garlic, chili flakes, and thyme. Sweat 2 minutes, then add the vegetables and stock, stir well, and bring to a simmer. Cover with a tight-fitting lid and transfer to the oven for 18 to 20 minutes or until the vegetables are tender. Discard the thyme and with a slotted spoon, remove the vegetables and place in a bowl tented with foil to keep warm. Place the saucepan over medium heat and reduce the stock by about two-thirds, for 10 to 12 minutes. Remove from heat and whisk in the diced butter and lemon juice. Salt to taste. Add the vegetables back to the sauce and return to low heat until they are warmed through and coated with the sauce.

Prepare the veal: Bring the veal to room temperature, season with salt and pepper, and rub with the thyme and rosemary. Heat a cast-iron skillet until very hot, then add the olive oil and swirl to coat. Sear the chops for 3 minutes per side for medium rare, or 4 minutes per side for medium. Let rest for 5 to 10 minutes, then slice from the bone and serve over the vegetables, drizzled with any extra sauce.

SERVES 3 TO 4

SMOKED GREEN WHEAT AND PARSNIPS

by **DAN BARBER, BLUE HILL AND BLUE HILL AT STONE BARNS**

When the ground freezes and the days are short, many markets shrink to barely half their summer size, but Chef Barber proves you can eat very well, even when some farmers have flown south for the winter. Here he relies on neither meat nor heated greenhouses, using modest stored grains and roots for a satisfying winter recipe that will make you hope asparagus takes a long winter's nap.

This dish is similar to a risotto, with two types of toothsome local grains taking the place of Arborio rice. The freekeh's subtle smokiness is balanced by an aromatic puree of parsnips and milk, so simple and satisfying you may want to serve it solo as a warming white soup on a dark winter's day.

Cook the grains: Heat the oil in a 4-quart saucepan over medium heat. Add the celery, carrot, and onion and sweat for about 5 minutes. Add the emmer and freekeh and toast for 2 minutes over low heat. Add 4 cups of water and the bay leaf and season well with salt and pepper.

Cover and simmer for 45 to 50 minutes, until the grains are tender with a bite. Remove the onion, celery, carrot, and bay leaf and discard. Strain the cooked grains through a mesh strainer set over a mixing bowl and reserve the cooking liquid. Return the grains to the saucepan and keep warm.

Grains

2 TABLESPOONS VEGETABLE OIL

1 STALK CELERY, HALVED CROSSWISE

½ PEELED CARROT

½ ONION, PEELED BUT NOT CHOPPED

1 CUP EMMER WHEAT

1 CUP FREEKEH

1 BAY LEAF

SALT AND FRESHLY GROUND BLACK PEPPER

Parsnips

1 TABLESPOON UNSALTED BUTTER

1 TABLESPOON OLIVE OIL

4 SMALL PARSNIPS, PEELED AND DICED, TO MAKE 1½ CUPS

1 GARLIC CLOVE

1 CUP MILK

2 TEASPOONS SHERRY WINE VINEGAR

1½ CUPS RESERVED GRAINS COOKING LIQUID OR STOCK

3 TABLESPOONS FINELY GRATED PARMESAN CHEESE, PLUS MORE TO TASTE

SALT AND FRESHLY GROUND BLACK PEPPER

(continued) ▶

Meanwhile, prepare the parsnip puree: Melt the butter and olive oil in a small saucepan over medium heat. Add the parsnips and garlic, season with salt and pepper, and sweat for 5 minutes. Add the milk and 1 cup of water and bring to a simmer. Cook gently for 20 to 25 minutes, until the parsnips are very soft. Transfer the parsnips and liquid to a blender, in batches if needed, and puree until smooth, 2 minutes. Adjust the consistency with 1 tablespoon water at a time if needed, until the puree is smooth and creamy.

To finish: Add the parsnip puree and sherry vinegar to the warm, cooked grains and return the heat to low. Adjust the consistency with the reserved grains' cooking liquid (or stock), starting with 1 cup, adding more if needed, until the mixture is creamy, smooth, and resembles a loose risotto. Remove from heat and stir in the Parmesan. Adjust seasoning with salt and pepper.

SERVES 8

GOLDEN BALL
TURNIPS

BEETS

HARUKEI
TURNIPS

COSMIC
PURPLE
CARROT

GOLDEN
BEETS

SCARLET
NANTES
CARROT

YELLOWSTONE
CARROT

PARSLEY
ROOT

CELERIAC

WATERMELON RADISH

HORSERADISH ROOT

Farmers MICHAEL AND MICHELLE BULICH
BULICH MUSHROOM CO.

A few Greenmarket farmers moonlight as forest foragers, sometimes offering a sudden score of spring morels, summer chanterelles, or fall porcini, all highly prized—and priced accordingly. The family behind Bulich Mushroom Farm is different. Their mushrooms are farmed, not wild, and as a result the Buliches offer one of the most reliable harvests around, no matter the month. As the days wax and then wane, asparagus is eclipsed by eggplant and peaches yield to pears, but year round, in sunshine and snow, this farmers market stand offers a steady supply of buttons, creminis, portobellos, oysters, and shiitakes.

They are the last of their kind, saved by city shoppers. New York State used to boast scores of mushroom farmers who, beginning in the 1950s, repurposed the obsolete ice houses that lined the Hudson River into mushroom farms growing the white button that's familiar in supermarkets and salad bars nationwide. But as massive mushroom operations sprouted in Pennsylvania and China, underselling New York growers, all but one went out of business.

Thankfully Frank Bulich, the second generation of Buliches to run the farm, had the prescience to note in the 1980s that there were many more interesting mushrooms than the white button, and that people, especially urbanites, had an appetite for them.

Frank experimented with portobellos, cremini (which are immature portobellos), and oysters and,

after decades in the wholesale trade, decided to take a chance selling directly to consumers shortly after the Union Square Greenmarket opened. Bulich mushrooms soon became a fixture. In a market at the mercy of the seasons, these mushrooms are immune to the annual fertile-fallow rhythms that mark local agriculture and eating. Rather, it's perpetual harvest.

> *Year round, in sunshine and snow, this stand offers a steady supply of buttons, creminis, portobellos, oysters, and shiitakes.*

Botanically neither plant nor animal, fungi favor darkness. After Frank's son, Michael, scatters millet-sized spores on stacked hemlock beds of manure, the fungi germinate in seventeen days and then yield two months of mushrooms.

While Michael tends the indoor beds, his wife, Michelle's, sunny smile welcomes customers at market: Every Wednesday and Saturday the criminis, oysters, shiitakes, portobellos, and, yes, white buttons are sold at Union Square within twenty-four hours of harvest, tucked fresh into plain brown paper bags. There's nothing wild or unpredictable about them, which is just the way the Buliches' customers like it.

◀ *Thirty years ago Frank Bulich saw that urbanites had an appetite for interesting mushrooms. His daughter-in-law Michelle still sells them within twenty-four hours of harvest.* (Amanda Gentile)

ROASTED MUSHROOMS WITH POACHED EGGS

by **RON LAPICO, JEAN-GEORGES**

This flexible dish can star any combination of cultivated button, oyster, portobello, crimini, or shiitake, or foraged wild mushrooms such as hen of the woods or, in late summer, chanterelle. Experiment with herbs as the months go by—parsley, thyme, chives, basil, dill, or even mint.

Without or without the egg, this recipe only takes a few minutes to cook up and is the kind of dish you could happily eat morning, noon, or night, year-round.

Fill a medium stockpot with water and add the white vinegar and salt and bring to a low simmer. Crack 1 egg into a shallow bowl. Swirl the water to create a vortex. Tip the egg into the center and simmer until the white is completely set and the yolk is warm and runny, 3 to 5 minutes. Remove with a slotted spoon and blot dry with a paper towel, and repeat the process with the second egg.

Heat the oil in a large sauté pan over medium-high heat until very hot. Add the mushrooms and sauté until caramelized but juicy, 3 to 4 minutes. Deglaze with the vinegar and reduce until dry, about another minute, then season gently with salt. Toss with fresh herbs.

Plate the mushrooms in two wide, shallow bowls, and arrange the poached eggs on top. Garnish with shaved Parmesan and salt, and finish with black pepper and olive oil. Serve with toast.

SERVES 2

¼ CUP WHITE VINEGAR

¼ CUP SALT

2 LARGE EGGS

2 TABLESPOONS OLIVE OIL

8 OUNCES OF MIXED MUSHROOMS CUT INTO 1-INCH PIECES

1 TABLESPOON SHERRY VINEGAR

2 TABLESPOONS CHOPPED, FRESH HERBS (SEE HEADNOTE)

SHAVED PARMESAN

SALT, FRESHLY GROUND BLACK PEPPER, AND OLIVE OIL TO TASTE

TOAST, FOR SERVING

CARROT PANCAKES WITH MAPLE PEARS

by **BILL TELEPAN, TELEPAN AND TELEPAN LOCAL**

Maple Pears

3 TABLESPOONS UNSALTED BUTTER, DIVIDED

2 CUPS DICED BOSC PEARS (FROM ABOUT 3 PEARS)

⅓ CUP MAPLE SYRUP

Chef Telepan became a market regular way back when he was at Gotham Bar and Grill twenty-five years ago, and he's remained one ever since. Today he's famous not only for his farm-to-white-tablecloth fare but also for getting great ingredients onto kids' cafeteria trays through the not-for-profit Wellness in the Schools.

But when it comes to getting people to eat vegetables, putting them in pancakes is about as enticing as it gets. Here cooked carrots are pureed with milk and eggs before being stirred into a batter that cooks up sweet. Follow Chef Telepan's method—letting each pancake set in the oven for a minute before returning to the stovetop—for easy flipping and perfect texture. The maple pears take it over the top, whether you're eating this dish for dessert or for breakfast. If it's the latter, you can boil the carrots the night before.

To prepare the maple pears: Melt 2 tablespoons of butter in a small saucepan over medium-high heat. Add the pears and sauté for 3 to 5 minutes to heat through and lightly soften. Add the maple syrup and the remaining butter, stirring gently to melt the butter and bring to a boil. Set aside.

Preheat the oven to 450°F.

To prepare the carrot pancakes: In lightly salted boiling water, cook the carrots until very tender, 10 to 12 minutes. Strain and run under cold water to cool them down.

Combine the cooked carrots and milk in a blender and puree until smooth. Add the eggs and orange zest to the blender and pulse until incorporated.

In a medium bowl, whisk together the flour, salt, sugar, baking powder, baking soda, and cinnamon, then pour in the carrot puree and stir to blend well. Fold in the grated raw carrots.

Melt 1 to 2 teaspoons of butter in an ovenproof sauté pan over medium heat. When the butter is bubbling, pour on ¼ cup of batter to form a pancake 4 inches in diameter. Depending on the pan size, you can cook a few pancakes at a time, but do not crowd the pan. When the pancake edges begin to turn brown, about 1 to 2 minutes, pop the pan into the oven until the surface is cooked, about 4 to 5 minutes. Return the pan to the stovetop, flip the pancakes over, and cook 2 more minutes over medium heat. If the pancakes are getting too dark, lower the heat on the stovetop.

Transfer the pancakes to a wire rack and repeat with the remaining batter.

Serve pancakes topped with warm maple pears.

Carrot Pancakes

12 OUNCES CARROTS, PEELED AND CUT INTO THIN SLICES, ABOUT 2 CUPS

1 CUP MILK

1 EGG

ZEST OF 1 ORANGE

1 CUP ALL-PURPOSE FLOUR

½ TEASPOON SALT

¼ CUP SUGAR

1 TEASPOON BAKING POWDER

½ TEASPOON BAKING SODA

1 TEASPOON GROUND CINNAMON

2 CUPS GRATED CARROTS

BUTTER FOR COOKING PANCAKES

Miller *DON LEWIS*
WILD HIVE FARM

It all began with a single bag of flour.

Don Lewis had been keeping bees and chickens his whole life when he heard about a farmer near him in the Hudson Valley who was growing organic animal feed. Don, who also baked to supplement his eggs and honey income, says he "ran up there" to buy grain for his birds. He was met with a surprise: In addition to the feed grain, the farmer, Alton Earnheart, had also grown an experimental patch of wheat for human consumption, and as luck would have it, Don pulled up on the day Alton had ground it into flour. "You're a baker," Alton said. "Maybe you could do something with this."

The farm was called Lighting Tree Farm, and that just-milled flour struck Don with an unforgettable bolt. "When I touched it," Don recalls, "I realized there was a world of difference between this and commercial flour. It had flavor! Terroir! I could taste the actual grain!"

Soon Don was buying as much flour as Alton could grow and grind, baking it into the scones, biscuits, pastries, and breads he sold at his Wild Hive stand at Union Square. But Don didn't just bake—he also immersed himself in studying the history of grain in New York State.

When Alton had asked area farmers about growing wheat, they'd laughed the idea off as if he'd proposed planting bananas. Widely forgotten was the fact that the Hudson Valley had once been the region's breadbasket. From the days of the Dutch, wheat and barley had been major crops there for more than two

◀ *Don didn't just bake. He immersed himself in grain history and soon mastered milling.*

centuries. Martha Washington herself wrote that she had to send for New York wheat to be able to bake a decent loaf of bread in Virginia.

But poor farming practices depleted the soil over the centuries, and when farmers moved west, they found that varieties that only grew 6 feet tall in the Northeast towered to 10 feet in the virgin ground of the Ohio Valley. The Industrial Revolution and the Erie Canal conspired so New York farmers abandoned their mills, and by the twentieth century, the only grains grown in New York were for animal feed.

So when Don stumbled upon a source of local flour, he first thought it would give him a niche in the marketplace. But the more he used—and learned—the more he realized that grain was such a fundamental ingredient, he didn't want to hide it under a bushel.

"Politics took over," he recalls of his evolving views. "I realized my children did not have access to the food I had access to when I was young, because of corporate domination of the food system. I said, 'It's ridiculous that you can't get a decent egg at the diner, and the pancakes are terrible.' I worked my way back and realized just how important grain was to this region. It was the mainstay of the community, and it had been completely lost. And I said, 'I'm gonna try to do something.' It was raising children into teenagers that helped me formulate that; I realized the example you make for your children is what you hope to get back."

Don worked with Alton to grow more grain, look for more seed, and expand his plantings and diversity; within a few years, Alton's yield increased from 5,000 pounds of flour to more than 25 tons, and from one variety to six, including rye, triticale, several wheat strains, and a flour corn—all of which Don bought and baked. Soon Don bought his own mills, too, and through time and trials, he mastered milling and came to understand the variables of speed, humidity,

temperature, and grain blend. He started selling small bags of flour first at Greenmarket, then wholesale, and then to larger and larger bakers.

The appetite for local grain grew, and now Don works with a half-dozen New York farmers who make more selling to him than they did growing commodity animal feed. Don has even grown a few test batches himself, including a heritage handful he brought back from the International Slow Food conference in Italy.

I realized there was a world of difference between this and commercial flour. It had flavor! Terroir! I could taste the actual grain!

Don now mills five days a week, and while that means he no longer has time to bake, his flour is sold from Manhattan to Albany, and his customers include top city chefs who are as taken with his flour as he was with that very first bag. His single biggest customer is Eataly, whose Manhattan outpost buys as much as Don can mill. The local farmers he buys from now grow more than a hundred acres of grain, but Don hopes to get that number up to 500 acres—and that he'll get competition as more New Yorkers are inspired to buy their own mills.

Don and his peers have worked "to get grains grown, processed, and distributed in this region. The farmers are happy, growing more acreage, getting a premium. It's about rebuilding the fundamentals of the food system and also making a decent living. I keep doing it because I believe in it. That's how I got here."

MAPLE WALNUT CARAMEL-CORN BALLS

by **JENNIFER KING, LIDDABIT SWEETS**

VEGETABLE OIL FOR GREASING

18 CUPS POPPED POPCORN
(ABOUT ⅔ CUP UNPOPPED
KERNELS)

8 TABLESPOONS (1 STICK)
UNSALTED BUTTER

¾ CUP GRANULATED SUGAR

¾ CUP FIRMLY PACKED LIGHT
BROWN SUGAR

¾ CUP MAPLE SYRUP,
PREFERABLY GRADE B

½ CUP LIGHT CORN SYRUP

1 CUP CHOPPED WALNUTS
(OPTIONAL)

1½ TEASPOONS BAKING SODA

1 TABLESPOON SALT

The alchemists at Brooklyn's Liddabit Sweets are famous for their craft approach to candy, and true to form their riff on popcorn balls benefits from a mapley makeover. Yes, you ideally should be equipped with an air popper and a candy thermometer, but otherwise it's easy—no mad scientist skills required.

Many farmers grow and sell ears of popping corn—buy at least two at a time so you can rub them together to remove the pointy little kernels, which keep indefinitely.

Grease two heatproof spatulas and one extra-large bowl. Place the popped popcorn in the bowl and set it aside.

Melt the butter in a medium saucepan over medium-high heat. Add the sugars, maple syrup, and light corn syrup, and using a heatproof spatula, stir to combine. Bring to a boil and insert the candy thermometer. Stirring often, cook the mixture to 290°F and stir in the walnuts, if using.

Remove the mixture from the heat, gently add the baking soda, and stir thoroughly. This will cause the mixture to foam slightly.

Carefully pour the hot caramel evenly over the popcorn and, using the spatulas, toss gently and constantly—like tossing a salad—until the popcorn is coated with caramel, about 1 minute. Add the salt and toss again. Then, using greased hands, shape the popcorn into balls (anywhere from tennis ball to softball-size) and place on sheet pans to cool.

BEET CAKE

by **KAREN DEMASCO, AUTHOR OF** *THE CRAFT OF BAKING*

Carrot cake may be the classic, but this cake takes its earthy sweetness from another root—beets. Sure, you can also whip it up with parsnips, carrots, or a combination, but straight beets are Chef DeMasco's favorite. Grated raw, they turn the batter a fuchsia hue, though the finished cake that emerges from the oven maintains only a demure pink tint, and your guests aren't likely to guess the defining ingredient.

Crème fraîche—a cultured dairy product slightly richer than sour cream—does double duty here. Mixed into the batter, it makes the cake wonderfully moist. Then, whipped with heavy cream, a finishing tangy dollop atop each slice perfectly balances the cake's subtle sweetness.

This recipe can also be used to make eighteen cupcakes; bake them for 20 to 25 minutes, using a toothpick to test for doneness as you would for the 8-inch cake.

Preheat the oven to 350° F.

Butter one 8-inch cake pan.

To make the cake: In the bowl of a stand mixer fitted with the paddle attachment, mix together the sugar, oil, vanilla, and crème fraîche on low speed until combined. Add the egg and yolk and increase to medium speed until well blended, about 30 seconds.

In a medium bowl, whisk together the flour, baking powder, baking soda, cinnamon, nutmeg, and salt. Add the flour mixture to the sugar mixture in three additions, mixing each time on low speed until combined. Add the grated beets all at once and mix on low speed until well incorporated, about 30 seconds. Scrape the sides to make sure everything is well mixed, then scrape the batter into the prepared pan and top with the reserved 2 tablespoons of sugar.

Beet Cake

1 CUP RAW OR DEMERARA SUGAR, PLUS 2 TABLESPOONS FOR TOPPING THE CAKE

½ CUP GRAPESEED OR OTHER NEUTRAL VEGETABLE OIL

¾ TEASPOON VANILLA EXTRACT

½ CUP CRÈME FRAÎCHE

1 EGG

1 EGG YOLK

1⅓ CUP ALL-PURPOSE FLOUR

1 TEASPOON BAKING POWDER

½ TEASPOON BAKING SODA

1½ TEASPOONS GROUND CINNAMON

¼ TEASPOON NUTMEG, IDEALLY FRESH GRATED

1¼ TEASPOON KOSHER SALT

2 CUPS GRATED BEETS, PACKED, FROM ABOUT 2 FIST-SIZED BEETS, 10 OUNCES IN WEIGHT, OR A COMBINATION OF BEETS, CARROTS, AND/OR PARSNIPS

Whipped Crème Fraîche Topping

½ CUP COLD, HEAVY CREAM

½ CUP CRÈME FRAÎCHE

2 TABLESPOONS CONFECTIONERS' SUGAR

(continued) ▶

Bake for 50 minutes to 1 hour, rotating the pan after 30 minutes and checking every 10 minutes after that, until the cake is golden, firm to the touch, and a cake tester comes out with crumbs, not wet batter. Cool the cake in the pan on a cooling rack. Once the cake is warm, not hot, remove it from the pan and let it finish cooling on the rack.

To make the topping: Combine the cold, heavy cream and crème fraîche in the bowl of a stand mixer with the whisk attachment. Whip on medium speed until the cream holds soft peaks. Sprinkle in the confectioners' sugar and whip on medium speed one minute more. Keep cool until ready to serve.

Serve the cake warm or at room temperature with a dollop of the crème fraîche–whipped cream on each slice.

MAKES ONE 8-INCH CAKE

Sugarmakers ANDY AND TONY VAN GLAD
WOOD HOMESTEAD

Quebec's forests may produce three-quarters of the world's maple syrup, but New Yorkers need not take off to the Great White North for their fix. The Empire State is home to many "sugarmakers" who tap wild maples each winter, including brothers Andy and Tony Van Glad, in the Catskills, who sell their maple syrup, maple candies, and maple sugar at city Greenmarkets year-round.

Every January the Van Glad brothers trudge out into the snowy forests to find sugar maples, drill holes, insert metal spouts, and hang metal buckets or plastic tubes. When late winter's nighttime temperatures remain below freezing but day readings inch up into the high 40s, the trees awaken from their dormancy and send sugar, in the form of sap, up from their roots and out to the buds. That's when the Van Glads work around the clock to collect sap and bring it back to their "sugarhouse" shack. Straight from the tree, maple sap looks and tastes like slightly sweet water, but boil it down and you'll be rewarded with liquid gold. Early in the season, it takes 40 to 50 gallons of sap to make a single gallon of syrup, which will have a light color and subtle flavor—designated as "Fancy" or "Grade A." As spring approaches and buds swell, sugar levels taper, and you'll need up to 80 gallons of sap to make one gallon of syrup, while the flavor and color intensify, resulting in the "Grade B" syrup that city customers line up for.

◄ *When winter nights are below freezing but days are warm, Andy collects sweet maple sap to boil down into syrup.* (Amanda Gentile)

APPLE CRISP WITH CORNMEAL TOPPING

by **DAVID LEBOVITZ, AUTHOR OF** *MY PARIS KITCHEN*

David Lebovitz has been transforming market fruit into sublime desserts for decades. After many years as pastry chef at Chez Panisse in Berkeley, he now bakes and writes in Paris. His book *Ripe for Dessert*, from which he once led a rhubarb-poaching demonstration at the Union Square Greenmarket, is the market-driven-sweets category killer, simmering and roasting its way through the harvest from apricots to winesaps.

Speaking of winesaps—for this crisp, use tart baking apples such as gala or jonagold, which have a bright flavor that's not too sweet and a firm flesh that doesn't collapse in the oven. And if you had the foresight to freeze raspberries, scatter them into the filling for a wonderfully jammy combination.

But no matter what you put in this crisp, you'll love what's *on* it. While most crisp toppings are little more than butter and sugar, Chef Lebovitz stirs in an ingredient that's as American as apple pie: cornmeal. Especially when stone ground, it gives this crisp a slightly sandy texture that's wonderful on everything from peaches to pears. Just be sure to leave the food processor running until the topping comes together into clumps, and tastes like cookie dough. If you make extra topping, you can freeze it—or eat it straight out of the bowl.

Preheat the oven to 375°F.

For the topping: In a food processor, pulse the flour, cornmeal, nuts, brown sugar, cinnamon, and salt. Add the butter and pulse until the mixture starts to form large clumps, about 30 seconds.

For the filling: Peel and core the apples and dice into 1-inch chunks. In a 2-quart baking dish, toss them with the sugar and vanilla extract.

Evenly distribute topping over the fruit. Bake for 45 to 50 minutes, until the apples are bubbling and cooked and the topping is deep golden brown.

SERVES 8 TO 10

Crisp Topping

¾ CUP ALL-PURPOSE FLOUR

⅔ CUP CORNMEAL

¾ CUP ALMONDS OR WALNUTS

½ CUP PACKED LIGHT OR DARK BROWN SUGAR

1 TEASPOON GROUND CINNAMON

PINCH OF SALT

½ CUP (1 STICK) COLD BUTTER, DICED INTO ½-INCH PIECES, PLUS MORE FOR GREASING THE PAN

Apple Filling

12 BAKING APPLES (ABOUT 4 POUNDS)

⅔ CUP SUGAR

1½ TEASPOONS VANILLA EXTRACT

Note: You can prepare the cornmeal crisp in advance and store in a zip-top freezer bag for a month or two, or refrigerate it for up to one week.

MAPLE BREAD PUDDING

by **SHARON BURNS-LEADER, BREAD ALONE**

For the Apples

3 TART APPLES

2 TABLESPOONS BUTTER

2 TABLESPOONS MAPLE SYRUP

PINCH OF MALDON SEA SALT

Bread Pudding

3 CUPS WHOLE MILK

1 VANILLA BEAN

6 EGG YOLKS

½ CUP SUGAR

¼ CUP BUTTER

6 CUPS OF CUBED BREAD,
SEE NOTE

PINCH OF MALDON SEA SALT

Maple Scotch Sauce

½ **CUP GRANULATED MAPLE SUGAR
(OR LIGHT BROWN SUGAR)**

¼ **CUP UNSALTED BUTTER**

½ **CUP MAPLE SYRUP**

½ **CUP HEAVY CREAM**

1 **TEASPOON BOURBON**

This can be made with brioche, challah, peasant bread, or even cubed croissants—no matter the building blocks, the rib-sticking results are rustic and rich.

You can make the maple-scotch sauce while the bread pudding is baking, or prepare it well ahead—covered in the refrigerator, it will keep for weeks.

Preheat the oven to 350°F.

Cook the apples: Core the apples and dice into one inch pieces. In a small skillet, melt the butter over medium-high heat. Add apples, maple syrup, and a pinch of salt and sauté for 4 to 5 minutes until heated through and softened. Remove from heat and set aside.

Make the pudding: Butter a 9x9" baking dish or two-quart casserole dish. Split the vanilla bean down the center and scrape out the seeds. In a mixing bowl, whisk the egg yolks, sugar, milk and vanilla bean (seeds) until blended. Place two-thirds of the bread chunks in the casserole dish, then add the apples and then, the remainder of the bread. Pour two-thirds of the custard over the bread and let it soak in, about 5 minutes. Press the bread to be sure that it has absorbed the custard, then pour the rest of the custard over. Bake in a water bath by placing your baking dish in a larger baking dish (lasagna pans are great for this!) and adding hot water to the larger, outer pan. Bake for 50-60 minutes or until the top is golden brown and the custard is just set. Carefully remove your baking dish from the hot water bath and cool on a rack.

Make the maple scotch sauce: Melt the maple sugar, butter and maple syrup together in a saucepan over medium heat. Once the sugar is dissolved, increase the heat to medium high and bring it to a boil. Cook for 5 minutes without stirring. Remove the pot from the heat and stir in the cream and the bourbon (do this carefully, it will sputter) and then stir in the salt.

Serve the bread pudding with a drizzle of the maple-scotch and vanilla ice cream.

SERVES 6 TO 8

DUSTY APPLE

by **JIM MEEHAN, AUTHOR OF** *THE PDT COCKTAIL BOOK*

4 OUNCES HOT APPLE CIDER

1 OUNCE AÑEJO TEQUILA

.75 OUNCE SUZE

1 DASH OF ANGOSTURA BITTERS

Americans love wine, beer, and cocktails, but this country was founded on another spirit: hard cider. In colonial times, every family tended apple trees that yielded fruits far too bitter and tannic to eat—but perfect to drink, in fermented form.

The temperance movement chopped down many an orchard, but fruit growers rebranded their increasingly sweet crop as something to snack on, and now when Americans speak of "cider" they don't mean the hard stuff.

Today many upstate orchardists are getting back into apple alcohol. And perhaps mixologist Meehan is winking at history with this tequila-kissed cocktail. Whether or not you raise a glass to the past, this drink goes down easy and warms you from the inside out.

Combine all ingredients in a prewarmed toddy glass. Garnish with grated cinnamon and a lemon wedge.

MAKES 1 COCKTAIL

HORSERADISH AQUAVIT

by **MARCUS JERNMARK, AQUAVIT NYC**

Aquavit Restaurant may be known for its haute Scandinavian cuisine, but the business takes its name from the most rustic drink in Northern Europe. These infused vodkas, literally called "water of life," aren't just an age-old way to preserve the harvest, they also ward off the chills in the formidable Nordic winter. The storied spirit has long been made with dill, but the Midtown restaurant drops all sorts of ingredients into vodka, offering flavorful thimblefuls of everything from strawberry and cucumber aquavits to plum, fennel, and beet. The recipe is always the same: Simply steep any fresh ingredient in vodka, tasting occasionally, until it is infused to your liking—anywhere from two days to one month.

This horseradish version is pretty magical. Most Americans know only the jarred, vinegary, "prepared" horseradish sometimes slathered on hot dogs, but the plant is awe-inspiring, growing up to 10 feet tall and sending down a gnarly white taproot that releases a powerfully aromatic oil when cut or grated. The chemical compound was evolved to deter animals from eating it, although humans have the opposite impulse. Drink it straight if you dare or in a bracing Bloody Mary.

ONE 1-LITER BOTTLE OF POTATO VODKA

2 OUNCES PEELED FRESH HORSERADISH, THINLY SLICED LENGTHWISE

Infuse the vodka with the horseradish for two to three weeks to desired depth of flavor.

MAKES 1 LITER

ACKNOWLEDGMENTS

When we decided to create a Greenmarket cookbook to celebrate our farmers, chefs, and customers, I envisioned a book that would allow people to cook like a Greenmarket chef—a book that might inspire some to join the food revolution started by a handful of intrepid farmers in a Manhattan parking lot some thirty years ago, and a book that acknowledges that the most important point in the journey from farm to table just might well be the kitchen. I'm proud to say I believe those goals were achieved within these pages.

But like everything we do at GrowNYC, this book is a collaborative effort and would not exist without the guidance and support of so many. I would like to thank our agent, Jennifer Unter, who helped guide this project from its very earliest stages; Renee Sedliar at Perseus, who took it on and helped shape our vision; Gabrielle Langholtz for her rich knowledge of food and farming in the Northeast—her devotion to the products our farmers grow shines through in her prose; Erin Merhar, Max Kelly, and Amanda Gentile, the team that, through the photographs they created, quite literally brought the dishes and our markets to life; and our dedicated and hardworking Greenmarket staff, including Michael Hurwitz, Cheryl Huber, Samantha Blatteis, and Jeanne Hodesh who painstakingly put the puzzle pieces of this book together. And like all projects at GrowNYC, we could not do our work without the support of our board members, especially our chair, Bob Kafin; our non-profit and corporate partners; and our funders.

Our deepest gratitude to those who welcomed us into their homes for photo shoots: Liz Carollo, Mary Cleaver and Ashley Hollister, Katia and Glenn Kelly, and Gabrielle Langholtz. And to James Oseland, whose love letter to the market sets the tone for these pages.

It's estimated that nearly 350,000 people walk through Union Square on a Friday in peak season. Early in the morning, a number of these patrons are chefs who have built their menus and restaurants around what the farmstands have to offer. Their interest in these local products, made obvious in the recipes in this book, has underscored the importance of supporting small family farms here in New York and created a dining trend that has changed the way America thinks about food. I cannot thank them enough for supporting our farmers and embracing GrowNYC's mission—and for elevating, day in and day out, what we all expect, demand, and desire from our food.

But without our farmers, this book and our plates would be empty. Their hard work, creativity, and dedication are awe-inspiring. Up before the crack of dawn, driving for hours, on their feet in the cold, the heat, the wind, then back the next day to do it all over again. By feeding us, they remind us that we rely on them and the earth to live. They, and the markets they create, fill our stomachs and revive our souls. They deserve our thanks, our praise, and, most of all, our patronage.

And, lastly, my thanks to you for buying this book. I hope you will cook from it and learn from it. By doing so, you will play a very important role in continuing GrowNYC's commitment to supporting family farms, improving the food supply, and educating the next generation of eaters in New York City and beyond. From everyone at GrowNYC, our sincerest thanks!

MARCEL VAN OOYEN
EXECUTIVE DIRECTOR, GROWNYC/GREENMARKET

HOW TO BE A SAVVY FARMERS MARKET SHOPPER

DON'T MAKE A SHOPPING LIST

Buy what inspires you and let that dictate your menu.

SHOP AROUND

Each stand has its own prices, growing practices, and quality standards. You'll quickly find your favorites.

GO EARLY

Unlike the grocery store, which is fully stocked one minute before closing, farmers plan to sell out by day's end, so early birds definitely catch the worm. And although tomatoes don't mind hours in the sun, lettuce does; what's not sold by the afternoon may well be wilted. (You can sometimes find great deals in the afternoon when farmers are eager to sell out and get home.)

TRY SOMETHING NEW

You may find foods you've never encountered, such as duck eggs, kohlrabi, fava beans, hardneck garlic, or chameh melon. If you only buy what you know, you will be missing out on some extraordinary taste experiences. Also, by buying these less-popular varieties, you encourage farmers to grow them. Although we generally think of extinction as something that happens to overharvested wild foods, it also happens to domesticated species that fall out of favor. By paying a farmer to grow that delicious old variety of lettuce or squash, you are helping ensure it will be around for generations to come.

DON'T REQUIRE THE "O" WORD

Plants and animals grown without synthetic chemicals are better for the environment and for eaters. But organic certification requires a lot of paperwork. Small farmers who sell direct may grow hundreds of crops, and the paperwork or expense of certification can be a burden. Still, small farmers are deeply and personally invested in the health of the land where they raise their families. Ask them how they farm. And if you prefer corn that hasn't been sprayed, don't be unhappy if you find the occasional worm.

BYO BAGS

Ditch the plastic. Cloth or canvas bags with shoulder straps let you load up.

KEEP COOL

Many markets offer great eggs, meat, fish, and dairy. If you pack a cooler or an ice pack, you won't have to rush home.

TALK TO STRANGERS

Sociology studies have shown that people are ten times as likely to talk to strangers at farmers markets as at supermarkets. So bring your kids, meet your neighbors, and make a morning of it.

LEARN TO PRESERVE

Local produce is only available in season. So load up and freeze or jar, and for the rest of the year feast on peach jam, tomato salsa, basil pesto, or frozen corn. The taste is beyond compare.

INDEX